janeva's kitchen
LOW CARB HOMESTYLE CLASSICS

JANEVA CAROLINE EICKHOFF

First Published in 2019 by
Janeva Eickhoff – Self-published
Janeva's Ideal Recipes®, Inc.
Janeva's Kitchen®
Copyright © 2019 Janeva Caroline Eickhoff

ISBN-13: 978-0-578-57617-6

The author is not a licensed physician, nutritionist, registered
dietician, practitioner, or medical professional and offers no medical
diagnoses, counseling, suggestions or treatments. The information
presented herein has not been evaluated by the U.S. Food and Drug
Administration (FDA), and is not intended to diagnose, treat, cure, or
prevent any disease. Full medical clearance from a licensed physician
should be obtained before beginning or modifying any diet, or
lifestyle program; inform your physician of all nutritional changes.

The author claims no responsibility to any person or entity for any
liability, loss or damage caused or alleged to be caused directly or
indirectly as a result of the use, application, or interpretation of the
information presented herein.

Photography by Pauline Boldt
Design and food styling by 26 Projects

Printed in Canada

For more information visit: www.janevaskitchen.com
contact@janevaskitchen.com

contents

eat well, live better.

— janeva

introduction

WELCOME TO THE LOW CARB LIFESTYLE

Whether you're new to the lifestyle or a seasoned veteran, I recommend that with any dietary change, you seek the advice of your doctor or a nutritionist who can help you along your way.

My back story regarding the low carb lifestyle started just over a decade ago. Over time as I aged, nearing my 50's, I found that carbohydrates were so much more challenging to digest. I was left with heartburn, belly bloat, weight gain, cravings, and even mental fogginess and depression. After researching for the right lifestyle to curtail and/or remove these issues, I found the low carb lifestyle to be a fit for me. The allowable foods were right up my alley – many low carb comfort food ingredients that were not only delicious but considered healthy!

Before embarking on this weight maintenance lifestyle, I knew I needed to shed some pounds; I tried just about every diet known to (wo)mankind. Nothing seemed to work for me until I learned my hairstylist lost 80+ lbs. using the Ideal Protein® weight loss program. It was then that I began their program, and much to my delight, I lost 33 lbs. in just 10 weeks. During my weight loss journey using the Ideal Protein® program, I realized that in order to make weight loss interesting and doable, I needed to create recipes that reminded me of the comfort foods I truly loved. So began the creation of those recipes and my first cookbook

was born – Janeva's Ideal Recipes. With the success of the cookbook and after my own weight loss, I embarked on a low carb diet to maintain all that hard work. Since then, I have been creating and developing low carb recipes for weight maintenance. This cookbook, Janeva's Kitchen, is not written for the Ideal Protein® weight maintenance program; it is my own journey of weight maintenance through the low carb lifestyle.

I believe that it is far easier to revise and remaster the comfort foods we love using low carb ingredients than it is to begin a new and completely different lifestyle using unfamiliar foods that leave us feeling deprived of our favorites. When I started writing this cookbook it was important to me to recreate those comfort foods by simply revising the ingredients and creating the same experience of enjoyment – but with far less carbs! I've remained as steadfast as I can by using every-day ingredients that may be purchased at your local grocers – and with this mindset, I've worked to create dishes the whole family will enjoy.

It is my great joy to present a personally created collection of recipes that are old-school favorites turned new-school comfort. I hope you truly enjoy the recipes and find many that will become your own family favorites.

– janeva

the low carb lifestyle

THE WHAT, THE WHY & THE HOW

WHAT IS IT?
the promise

You don't need to eliminate all the foods you love to maintain a healthy weight.

Living the low carb lifestyle simply means reducing carbohydrates in your meals and snacks. By avoiding starches and sugars, blood sugar tends to stabilize, reducing the level of fat-storing insulin in the body.

Carbohydrates are the body's primary resource for energy. Once those carbs are depleted, the body burns stored fats instead, resulting in a balance of weight maintenance (if consuming a moderate amount of carbs.)

what can you eat?

Anything from meats and fish, to vine veggies, to select fruits and healthy fats – even desserts! High-carb foods like sugar, rice, pasta, beans, potatoes and breads would need to be eliminated. Or, better yet, substitute lower carb alternatives. That's where I come in!

I have worked years to create low-carb comfort foods using ingredients that maintain the comfort, taste and goodness we all know and love. The recipes in this cookbook are every bit as rich, luscious, and flavorful as the standard high carb classics of the past.

WHY FOLLOW IT?
the benefits

When your days are filled with energy and clarity, you'll find you get a lot more out of eating a little less.

According to the Mayo Clinic, "Low-carb diets may help prevent serious health conditions such as metabolic syndrome or diabetes and reduce high blood pressure and cardiovascular disease.

Almost any diet that helps you maintain a healthy weight can reduce or even reverse risk factors for cardiovascular disease and diabetes."

www.mayoclinic.org/healthy-lifestyle

I have personally benefited from avoiding high-carb starches and sugars. As a result, I find I have:

- Fewer food cravings
- Higher energy
- Satiated appetite
- Better sleep
- Better mental clarity
- Fewer mood swings
- A more consistent body weight
- Fewer to no hot flashes (in the menopause years)

HOW DO I DO IT?
the lifestyle

Living the low carb lifestyle is a rewarding journey; there are factors you will learn making it possible to succeed (see pg. 12).

Currently, the definition of exactly what constitutes a *low carb lifestyle* is unclear. Your *low* may not be *low* for someone else.

Your optimal carb intake depends on your age, gender, genetics, activity level, personal preferences, food culture, body composition and overall metabolic health.

here's how I do it

01 ─────────────

Download a food diary app such as MyFitnessPal. In the app, enter all the parameters mentioned previously such as age, gender, etc. The app will help guide you through the process and analyze how many calories, carbs and percentage of macros you should be consuming to maintain your weight.

note: A macro is short for macronutrients, which refers to the three key food groups our bodies need to function well:

- Carbohydrates - which provide energy
- Fats - which provide brain and organ function and appetite
- Protein - which repairs, protects, and builds muscle

02 ─────────────

Use the app to input your daily food consumption. Continue to track every meal, snack, and beverage each day. Soon, it will become habit. Doing this will keep you on track and teach important skills for maintaining. In time, you may no longer need the app as the low carb lifestyle becomes second nature.

03 ─────────────

Carbs vs. Net Carbs: You will be counting 'net' carbs rather than total carbs in a dish.

WebMD defines the concept as such: "Net carbs [are] based on the principle that not all carbohydrates affect the body in the same manner.

Some carbohydrates, like simple or refined starches and sugars, are absorbed rapidly and have a high glycemic index, meaning they cause blood sugar levels to quickly rise after eating. Excess simple carbohydrates are stored in the body as fat. Examples of these foods include potatoes, white bread, white rice, and sweets.

Other carbohydrates, such as the fiber found in whole grains, fruits, and vegetables, move slowly through the digestive system, and much of it isn't digested at all (insoluble fiber)."

www.webmd.com/women/features/net-carb-debate#1

HOW TO CALCULATE NET CARBS

When calculating daily carbs, calculate the total based on 'net' carbs.

TOTAL CARBS (grams)
—
FIBER (grams) + SUGAR ALCOHOL (grams)
=
NET CARB (grams)

Note: Sugar alcohols have already been deducted for the net carb count in the recipes in this cookbook.

SUMMARY

All the recipes in this cookbook are considered low carb. You will find a variety of LCHF (low carb/high fat) and LCLF (low carb/low fat). An effort should be made to balance LCHF with LCLF meals throughout the week. LCHF meals, drinks, and snacks are those typically made with dairy fats such as cheese, heavy cream, cream cheese, and sour cream. LCLF meals use healthier fats such as olive oil, avocado, or coconut oils, if any at all. This cookbook and the recipes within it are meant to give you choice and variety during your journey. As with any lifestyle, balance should be the goal.

The low-carb lifestyle is not only tasty but rewarding. It is a personal passion to create some of the best dishes you've ever tasted with hopes they will also become your family favorites. You won't feel deprived and you can always find an alternative for the comfort foods you love.

I hope you enjoy living the low-carb lifestyle!

Cheers,

janeva

nutritional disclaimer

The information we provide at Janeva's Kitchen is not intended to replace consultation with a physician, nutritionist, dietician or other medical professional qualified to answer any questions you may have regarding dietary changes and/or your own medical condition.

For questions or concerns about any medical conditions you may have, or any dietary changes you may make to your lifestyle, consult with a professional.

The content provided is not intended to be relied upon for medical diagnosis or treatment. Do not disregard medical advice or delay visiting a medical professional because of something you read here or through our other communication channels and/or social media sites.

As a courtesy, nutrition info is provided for each recipe and has not been reviewed by a medical professional or dietary organization. Total carb count excludes sugar alcohols; net carb count excludes both sugar alcohols and fiber. We have done our best to provide the accuracy of nutritional information for each recipe – you are welcome to make your own calculations.

in the pantry

PROTEIN

Most of my proteins are purchased from Costco; I find they are simply the best in freshness, flavor, and tenderness – a  great budget saver too. After coming home with my bounty of bulk proteins, I vacuum seal them in 1 lb. portions and freeze for future meals. We have a ridiculous amount of refrigerator/freezer space in our home; on the upside, I can store several varieties of protein in the freezer.

bacon

Many brands of bacon can be loaded with sugar; always check the ingredients. I like to purchase bacon at a local butcher where I am assured it's fresh and free of added sugar. I stock both thick cut and regular cut.

bulk pork sausage

Jimmy Dean® brand is my favorite bulk sausage, as I find it has the best flavor. I often stock a few tubes in the freezer to have on hand when needed.

chicken

All parts of the chicken are good for stocking – breasts, thighs, wings and drumsticks. Skin on, skin off, bone-in, boneless, you name it – it's in our freezer. I am also fond of the deli rotisserie chickens; they're perfect for dishes requiring cooked chicken. Be aware of any added sugar in the brine.

eggs

Always use large eggs in recipes unless the recipe mentions otherwise. Eggs are used throughout this cookbook in savory dishes as well as baked goods. I always keep fresh eggs in the fridge; they're the perfect low carb/high protein food.

fish and seafood

Always best fresh but frozen will do in a pinch. I like to have shrimp on hand, especially for the Alfredo dish in this cookbook. Shrimp cocktail makes a perfect high protein, low carb snack. Tilapia is a white firm fish that we enjoy as well as walleye. Either of these works well in the fish recipes in this cookbook.

ground beef

I always purchase the 93% lean, unless a specific recipe calls for a higher fat ground beef. I do have a few recipes in the cookbook requiring ground beef with a higher fat content, as I find it necessary in some dishes. I strive to purchase grass fed beef which is typically leaner and provides key nutrients not found in standard ground beef.

salmon

Wild caught or farm-raised? Farm raised salmon is pale orange in color and most commonly served in restaurants; wild caught is reddish in color and some folks prefer its leaner reputation. I use the farm raised salmon, as I find it better tasting and more budget friendly.

turkey

Ground turkey comes in handy to use in place of ground beef in recipes if you're looking for a lower fat protein addition to a dish; however, turkey is much leaner than beef and requires a heavier hand with seasonings for the best flavor.

DAIRY

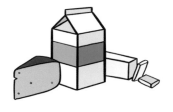

My refrigerator is always full of variety when it comes to dairy products. In general, full fat dairy products are low in carbs – however, always check the label to be sure no unnecessary sugars or other high carb ingredients have been added.

butter (salted and unsalted)

When a recipe doesn't designate salted or unsalted butter, either may be used. I like to keep both unsalted and salted in my fridge as I find they both serve their unique purpose in recipes. Throughout this cookbook, I use both.

shredded cheeses

Mozzarella, parmesan and cheddar are staples and the most widely used varieties – perfect for topping casseroles, eggs and more.

block cheeses

if you like cheese, a block of cheese is great to have for cutting off a few slices for a snack. Laughing Cow® cheese is a nice portable snack on-the-go. Have a watchful eye for the carbs in cheeses and always check the nutrition label.

string cheese

Perfect for snacking.

cream cheese

I find this product a treasure and always stock it in my fridge. Perfect for both sweet and savory dishes, I use cream cheese throughout this cookbook.

half & half

Great for coffee creamer and delicious poured over fresh berries for a low carb treat. Be sure to count carbs; they are higher in half & half than in fuller fat heavy whipping cream.

heavy whipping cream

Great for coffee creamer, desserts, and plenty of other dishes in this cookbook, heavy whipping cream is a staple ingredient in my fridge.

note: There is a difference between heavy cream and heavy whipping cream -- heavy cream has higher fat content than heavy whipping cream and may also be used for the low carb lifestyle. I use heavy whipping cream because it's easier to find in stores and works well for its purposes.

nut milks

While almond and cashew milk are nut milks and not dairy milks, they are most often available in the refrigerated dairy section. I like having both varieties in my fridge but one or the other is fine. I find them perfect for smoothies or even coffee creamer during days when I want to eat/drink a bit leaner (than using heavy creamers). Be sure to purchase unsweetened for the lowest carbs.

sour cream

Sour cream is a great topper for eggs, casseroles, chili or stews, veggies, or Mexican dishes. I also use sour cream in the scones recipe for added moisture.

BAKING

Low carb baked goods are the most challenging foods to recreate as the base ingredients are entirely different (almost) from standard baked goods ingredients. Therefore, the end results should be entirely different, yes? Yes and no. Yes, they will be different; however, I've worked very hard to create baked goods that are worthy in taste and texture as compared to the standard baked goods we all know and love. No, they're not entirely different; I find them slightly different.

The good news is that we get baked goods in a low carb lifestyle, and I can live with that difference!

That's meaningful. Subbing ingredients such as sugar substitutes, flours, etc. is not recommended as it will drastically change the results of the flavor and texture of the baked goods. I recommend stocking the baked goods pantry items that are listed here.

baking powder / baking soda

Both are required for baked goods recipes in this cookbook. Watch the expiration date, or they will become inadequate in doing their job!

blanched almond flour

The only kind of almond flour I use in this cookbook is the blanched, finely ground almond flour. I like using Costco Kirkland® or Bob's Red Mill® brands.

coconut flour

Used very little in this cookbook but necessary for some recipes, I use Bob's Red Mill® brand. Coconut flour is very different than almond flour and they should not be subbed one for the other.

SWEETENERS

There are a wide variety of low carb sweeteners and sugar substitutes on the market. I've tried every single one, whether granular or liquid, and now use only the sweeteners listed below:

allulose (granular)

This is by far my favorite granular sweetener, and I use it in most of the baked goods and dessert recipes in this cookbook. Not familiar with allulose? Here are some facts from allulose.org:

1. Allulose is a natural sweetener found in figs, jackfruit, raisins and dates.

2. It is not a sugar-alcohol based sweetener and therefore is gastrointestinal tolerant.

3. Allulose is 1:1 to regular sugar for substitution.

4. Allulose is low in calories and absorbed by the body, but not metabolized, and is non-glycemic; that is, it has no effect on blood glucose. Perfect for low carb, diabetic and keto diets. For more information on allulose, visit www.allulose. org.

erythritol
confectioners, granulated and brown sugar

Erythritol is a sugar-alcohol based sweetener. When used in baking, it can create a cooling 'arctic effect' in the mouth which I find off-putting – for this reason I don't use it in most of my baked goods. With that said, it does have merit in some recipes in this cookbook.

liquid stevia

This sweetener is perfect for sweetening recipes that don't require the bulk of granulated sugar. I use this for adding sweetness to smoothies.

Splenda® (granular)

Splenda does well in baked goods that need to be light and airy. I use it in only a few recipes for that reason.

THICKENERS
xanthan gum

Xanthan gum is an effective thickening agent and stabilizer to prevent ingredients from separating. I use this in some baked goods to keep them from crumbling after baking.

glucomannan

Made from the konjac root, glucomannan is an excellent thickener when used in soups and stews. A little bit goes a long way; follow recipe directions for use.

OTHER
stevia sweetened chocolate chips

I use Lily's® brand chocolate chips for all my baked goods and other recipes requiring chocolate chips. They store easily in the freezer.

nuts

There is always a variety of nuts stored in my

freezer including almonds, pecans, macadamias, peanuts, sunflower and walnuts for baking and low carb snacking.

nut butters

Peanut and almond butter are essential ingredients in my pantry; both are used for baked goods and smoothies. A small spoonful as a snack works well too.

oils

My cabinets are filled with oils because I enjoy oils flavored with herbs and spices, and I use different oils for baking, cooking and salads. My every day essentials are:

- Avocado oil
- Liquid coconut oil
- Olive oil (mild and extra virgin)

unsweetened cocoa powder

Used in baking, drinks and smoothies or for flavoring recipes with chocolate.

vanilla extract

Use only pure (not imitation) vanilla extract for the best flavor. Sometimes I use clear vanilla extract, so it won't tint foods such as a sweetened whipped cream.

whey protein powder

I stock vanilla and chocolate flavored protein powders and use them in baking and smoothies.

FRESH PRODUCE

I love a fresh bounty of fruits and vegetables in my fridge. Here are the staples that rotate in and out of there depending on planned meals for the week.

FRUITS	VEGGIES		FRESH HERBS
Avocado	Asparagus	Jalapeno	Italian parsley
Blackberries	Baby bella mushrooms	Jicama	Basil
Blueberries	Bell peppers	Lettuce – romaine, butter, red & green	Chives
Lemons	Broccoli		Cilantro
Limes	Brussels sprouts	Rhubarb	Dill
Peaches	Cauliflower	Spaghetti squash	Thyme
Raspberries	Celery	Spinach (fresh)	
Strawberries	Celery root	Turnips	
Tomatoes – baby, whole, Roma and heirloom	Green beans	Yellow onions	
	Green onion	Yellow squash	
		Zucchini	

a bit of historical trivia

SILVER SPOONS, CRYSTAL PLATES + THE FARM CHAIR

by Joanne Eickhoff

It was time to photograph the recipes, and after cleaning out my own china hutches and buffets on a search for just the right food props, I asked my mother what she might have at her home that could also work as props. Much to my amazement, she had several items which have been used in the photos you'll see throughout this cookbook. These family food props have some interesting stories I'd like to share with you. I've asked my mother to write a little historical blurb behind the pieces used in some of the photos, and here are her words...

— janeva

silver spoons

There is a human-interest story behind the silver spoons displayed in several photographs in Janeva's cookbook. In the 1840's, several years before the beginning of the Civil War, my great, great uncle (Janeva's great, great, great uncle) lived with his wife on a large farm in Kentucky. They built a very nice home which I had the privilege of visiting several years ago. My great, great uncle gave his wife a large silver set as a gift. Each piece of the silver set was engraved with their initials. During the Civil War this set of silver was buried underground to protect it from being stolen by marauders coming through the area. My great, great uncle was not a believer in slavery and so was sympathetic to the Yankees from the north. Anyone working for him on his farm was a free man provided with decent living conditions, food and a stipend. These workers were free to leave his employment at any time. Most chose to stay, and those who did were remembered in my great, great uncle's will. Following the war, the silver set was removed from underground. Eventually it was divided and then divided again among relatives. I received a fruit bowl and several spoons from my father's share of the silver set. These items are now approximately 170 years old. I have actual letters written by my great, great uncle which verify the story. Most of these letters were written to, and received from, his brothers and are quite fragile, but still legible, after all these years.

crystal plates

Scattered throughout Janeva's cookbook, photographs will show her food being displayed on crystal plates. These plates are Cambridge crystal. The pattern is Caprice. During our first year of marriage (1953), my husband (Janeva's father) and I received a set of these crystal goblets as a Christmas gift from my parents, Janeva's grandparents. When we tried to add more pieces to what eventually became our crystal collection, we discovered that late in the 1950's the crystal was no longer available for purchase. Thus began years of visiting flea markets, antique stores and garage sales with the hope of adding unusual pieces of Cambridge crystal to our collection. We were quite successful in our efforts. I now have 3 china cabinets in my home, plus my high-up kitchen cabinets, overflowing with the results of our efforts. What fun to see pieces of our Cambridge crystal featured in Janeva's Kitchen!

farm chair

The chair pictured in this cookbook belonged to my parents, Janeva's grandparents. The chair has been in the family for as long as I can remember, making it over 80 years old. This particular chair was always referred to by my family as 'the kitchen chair.'

My mother had a white table with an enameled surface in her kitchen; this chair was tucked under that table when not in use by my mother. She was the only person who used the chair on a regular basis, since the family meals were eaten in the dining room of our farmhouse where a dining room chair was available for each family member.

I am now the owner of the chair and use it on a daily basis. It is an extremely sturdy chair, made of oak, and still shows no signs of deterioration — for instance, no wobbly legs and no loose joints. Even the finish on the chair is original and has withstood the test of time.

Bread & Breakfast

contents

Blender Pancrepes

SERVINGS: 3
(2 pancrepes per serving)

Pancakes + Crepes = Pancrepes. After many, many trials to create the perfect low carb pancake-crepe, this one exceeds all! They are rich, tender and silky. Top them with a dollop of whipped cream and mixed berries or mashed peaches; butter and sugar free pancake syrup work just as well. You can't go wrong either way, and this recipe couldn't be any easier. Kids love them too!

INGREDIENTS

pancrepes

1 T. unsweetened vanilla almond or cashew milk

2 large eggs

1 tsp. vanilla extract

2 oz. cream cheese, softened and cut in cubes

2/3 C. blanched almond flour

2 T. allulose granular sugar substitute

1 tsp. baking powder

Cooking spray

toppings (optional)

Whipped Cream, pg. 264

Berries of choice

Mashed peaches

Butter and sugar free pancake syrup

DIRECTIONS

1. In order, place almond milk, eggs, vanilla and cream cheese in a blender. Blend on high until creamy, about 15 seconds.

2. Add remaining ingredients. Blend until smooth.

3. Heat a griddle or large skillet to medium heat; coat with cooking spray.

4. Pour batter onto skillet making 6 pancrepes. I use a standard size ice cream scoop to measure and pour the pancrepe batter onto the skillet. Cook until the pancrepes start to bubble on top, about 3 minutes. Flip to other side for about 30 seconds to finish cooking; serve.

janeva's tips

A thin metal spatula works perfectly to easily flip these pancrepes. Thicker plastic spatulas make it more challenging to get under the pancrepe without turning it into an abstract art piece.

NET CARBS 3g (per serving, no toppings)				
calories	fat	protein	carbs	fiber
282	23g	11g	14g	11g

Blue Ribbon Bread

SERVINGS:

24 dinner or sandwich buns
12 bagels or breadsticks

one dinner or sandwich bun; double the nutrition info if consuming one bagel or breadstick

The most versatile bread recipe and incredibly delicious! Make dinner buns, bagels, sandwich buns and breadsticks with this dough. Serve them plain or sprinkle with your favorite seasonings such as Everything bagel seasoning, red pepper flakes, garlic powder, Italian seasoning, toasted sesame seeds, etc.

INGREDIENTS

3 C. blanched almond flour

1 T. baking powder

4 oz. cream cheese, softened

5 C. finely shredded mozzarella cheese

4 large eggs

DIRECTIONS

1. Preheat oven to 400 degrees.

2. In a medium mixing bowl, whisk together almond flour and baking powder.

3. Add flour mixture and remaining ingredients to a food processor or electric mixing bowl with a dough blade and mix; batter will be stiff.

4. See below for 4 different bread variations using this dough. Bake all variations for 15 – 17 minutes or until lightly browned.

VARIATIONS

1. **Dinner Buns** – Using a standard ice cream scoop, scoop batter onto a parchment lined baking sheet making 24 buns.

2. **Sandwich Buns** – Using a standard ice cream scoop, scoop batter onto a parchment lined baking sheet making 24 buns. Using the bottom of a flat drinking glass, lightly moisten with water and press down on dough balls to flatten for hamburger or sandwich-style buns.

3. **Bagels** – Place 2 scoops of dough onto a work surface; using both palms, roll into an 8" inch log shape and form into a circle pressing ends together. Makes 12 bagels.

4. **Breadsticks** – Place 2 scoops of dough onto a work surface, roll into an 8" inch log shape and place on baking sheet. Makes 12 breadsticks.

NET CARBS 2g - *per serving				
calories	fat	protein	carbs	fiber
152	10g	12g	4g	2g

Blueberry Scones

SERVINGS: 12

Blueberries always remind me of my childhood, and these scones are truly comfort food for me. Growing up with a summer cabin in Minnesota, we found an expansive wild blueberry patch deep in the woods. After picking four 1-gallon ice cream buckets full of blueberries, the blueberries were used to make ice cream, pancakes, jam and desserts; or, we would just eat them plain in a bowl with heavy cream and sugar. I find this scone recipe better than the standard ingredient scones you might purchase at a coffee shop. I hope you enjoy them as much as I do!

INGREDIENTS

2 C. blanched almond flour

¼ C. coconut flour

2 ½ T. allulose granular sugar substitute

1 T. baking powder

¼ tsp. salt

2 large eggs

2 T. sour cream

2 T. heavy whipping cream

1 tsp. vanilla extract

1 C. fresh blueberries

DIRECTIONS

1. Preheat oven to 325 degrees.

2. In a large bowl, add dry ingredients. Stir with a whisk to mix.

3. Add wet ingredients (except blueberries). Stir with a rubber spatula to mix; batter will be stiff.

4. Add blueberries and gently fold into batter without crushing berries.

5. On a parchment lined work surface, place batter in the center and pat down to a 10" x 8" rectangle. (Lightly moist hands work best for patting down; I run hands under water and shake excess water.)

6. Using a large knife, cut into 6 equal squares, then cut each square diagonally to make 12 scones.

7. Using a spatula, carefully move scones onto a large parchment lined baking sheet.

8. Bake 20 - 25 minutes or until lightly golden and done. Transfer to a cooling rack and let cool before consuming or they will taste dry. Once cooled, they are moist and delicious!

NET CARBS 4g - per serving				
calories	fat	protein	carbs	fiber
163	12g	6g	7g	3g

Chocolate Zucchini Muffins

SERVINGS: 9

Zucchini makes magic by providing a super moist muffin – a perfect way to sneak in some veggies too. The delicate texture and rich dark chocolate make these Chocolate Zucchini Muffins taste more like cupcakes. Cupcakes for breakfast? Yes, please.

INGREDIENTS

1 C. shredded zucchini (unpeeled)

½ C. coconut flour

½ C. allulose granular sugar substitute

¾ tsp. baking soda

2 T. unsweetened cocoa powder

¼ tsp. salt

½ tsp. cinnamon

1 tsp. instant espresso granules

¼ tsp. xanthan gum

3 eggs, room temp

2 tsp. vanilla extract

1 T. olive or avocado oil

¼ C. heavy whipping cream

1/3 C. stevia chocolate chips (I use Lily's)

Cooking spray

DIRECTIONS

1. Preheat oven to 350 degrees.

2. Place shredded zucchini in a microwave proof bowl. Heat on high 20 seconds; lightly blot with paper towels to absorb moisture. Set aside.

3. To a large bowl, add dry ingredients (except chocolate chips); stir with a whisk to blend.

4. To a separate bowl, add wet ingredients. Using a stand mixer or electric hand mixer, blend until creamy. Add dry ingredients to wet ingredients, and blend until mixed. Stir in chocolate chips.

5. Spray a 12-cavity muffin tin (or use parchment paper liners). Using a standard ice cream scoop, place a level scoop of batter into muffin tin making 9 muffins. Sprinkle additional chocolate chips on top, if desired.

6. Bake 25 – 30 minutes, or until an inserted toothpick comes out clean.

7. Cool completely on cooling rack.

janeva's tips

These muffins freeze well wrapped and stored in an airtight container. I make them in double batches to have on hand for a quick breakfast on-the-go or an afternoon snack.

NET CARBS 6g - per serving				
calories	fat	protein	carbs	fiber
134	9g	4g	10g	4g

Cinnamon Roll Muffins

SERVINGS: 12

Everything you love about a good cinnamon roll, but ready in a fraction of the time. I like to make fast and easy recipes without compromising on taste or texture. Cinnamon rolls are one of my favorite weekend breakfasts, and when I want something quick, these do the trick! No need to fiddle around rolling out dough and cutting into rolls; simply stir up the batter and scoop into a muffin tin. They are very easy to make and even better to eat!

INGREDIENTS

rolls

1 ½ C. blanched almond flour

2 tsp. baking powder

2 oz. cream cheese, softened

2 ½ C. shredded mozzarella cheese

2 large eggs

streusel

½ C. brown sugar alternative, loosely packed (I use Sukrin® Gold or Swerve®)

1 ½ T. salted butter, melted

1 ½ tsp. cinnamon

½ C. chopped pecans

glaze (optional)

Cream Cheese Glaze, pg. 242

DIRECTIONS

1. Preheat oven to 350 degrees.

2. To a medium bowl, add all streusel ingredients; stir with a fork until butter is well incorporated. Set aside.

3. To a large mixing bowl, add almond flour and baking powder; stir until blended. Add remaining roll ingredients and mix until blended.

4. Using ½ the streusel mixture, add to muffin batter and gently fold. (You will not want to completely combine, just fold until the entire batter is marbled with streusel.)

5. Line a standard size 12-cavity muffin tin with parchment baking liners. Using a standard size ice cream scoop, scoop batter into tin, making 12 muffins. (If liners are not available, spray tin with cooking spray before adding batter.)

6. Sprinkle remaining half of streusel mixture evenly over the top of muffins.

7. Bake 15 minutes. Remove muffin tin from oven and place on a cooling rack. Cool muffins 15 minutes in pan.

8. Drizzle with Cream Cheese Glaze, if desired.

janeva's tips

Cooling the muffins before eating is recommended; low carb baked goods will taste dry right out of the oven and will moisten as they cool. These muffins freeze well and reheat well in the microwave. If the glaze is not used, try spreading a warmed muffin with salted butter – delicious!

NET CARBS 2g (per serving)				
calories	fat	protein	carbs	fiber
212	17g	11g	4g	2g

Cinnavanilla Baked Peaches

SERVINGS: 2

I look forward to peach season each year and like to purchase them from an organic roadside stand or outdoor farmers market. This recipe was created based on the memory of eating and enjoying peaches mixed with cottage cheese as well as high-carb peach cobbler recipes of the past. Combining those memories, I've created an elevated dish to make a healthy, elegant, but easy recipe that is simply one of my favorite breakfasts; however, these baked peaches may also be eaten as a snack or dessert... and finding a delicious dessert that is high in protein and 10g or less net carbs, that's a win!

INGREDIENTS

1 fresh peach, halved and pit removed

1 T. unsalted butter

2 tsp. brown sugar substitute (I use Sukrin Gold® or Swerve®)

2/3 C. small curd 4% milkfat cottage cheese

1/8 tsp. cinnamon

¼ tsp. vanilla extract

2 T. chopped pecans

DIRECTIONS

1. Preheat oven to 350 degrees.
2. Place peach halves cut side up in a baking dish. Divide the butter and brown sugar substitute evenly, and top each peach half. Bake 12-14 minutes.
3. Meanwhile, add cottage cheese, cinnamon and vanilla extract to a small bowl. Stir to mix.
4. Evenly top baked peach halves with cottage cheese mixture and sprinkle with pecans. Serve warm or chilled.

janeva's tips

This recipe may easily be doubled (or more) for extra servings. To cut and pit a peach, place peach on a steady work surface. Find the natural seam that runs end-to-end and insert a paring knife. Follow the seam with the knife and cut the peach through to the pit all the way around. Hold peach in your hands and twist to separate from the pit. Run a spoon around edge of pit to cut the flesh and scoop out pit.

NET CARBS 10g (per serving)				
calories	fat	protein	carbs	fiber
158	9g	10g	11g	1g

Cornbread Muffins

SERVINGS: 10

Using high carb corn meal in standard cornbread recipes lends a coarse texture to the cornbread. In this recipe, substituting low carb flaxseed meal does the same. The recommended cornbread extract amps up the flavor making a similar tasting cornbread to the one we know and love. I serve these muffins warmed with salted butter and drizzled with sugar free honey or maple syrup – they make a great accompaniment to the Kalua Pork & Cabbage recipe, pg. 170.

INGREDIENTS

cornbread

2 C. blanched almond flour

¼ C. flaxseed meal

½ tsp. baking soda

¼ tsp. salt

2 T. sour cream

3 T. heavy whipping cream

1 T. water

3 large eggs

1 tsp. *cornbread or butter extract

3 T. unsalted butter, melted

toppings (optional)

Sugar free honey or sugar free maple syrup, to taste

Salted butter, to taste

DIRECTIONS

1. Preheat oven to 350 degrees.

2. To a large mixing bowl, add dry ingredients. Stir to mix.

3. Add liquid ingredients (except butter) to dry ingredients, and stir until blended.

4. Slowly add melted butter to batter while stirring to blend (to prevent cooking eggs).

5. Line a 12-cavity muffin tin with 10 parchment baking liners. If you don't have liners, spray tin with cooking spray. Using a standard size ice cream scoop, place one scoop batter into each baking liner, making 10 muffins.

6. Bake 18 - 20 minutes or until an inserted toothpick comes out clean.

7. Serve with salted butter and sugar free honey or maple syrup, if desired.

janeva's tips

*Cornbread extract is not commonly found in grocery stores but is available online, and I highly recommend it for the best flavor. I purchase the extract on Amazon; there are several brands to choose from that work well.

NET CARBS 2g (per serving)				
calories	fat	protein	carbs	fiber
228	20g	7g	5g	3g

Mug
Pancakes

SERVINGS: 6
(2 mug pancakes per serving)

Have the desire for pancakes but don't want the fuss of making them over the stove top? Then this recipe is the one for you. The batter may be made the night before and stored in fridge for a lightning quick breakfast the next morning. Make them in batches, and freeze for another meal.

INGREDIENTS

mug pancakes

4 large eggs

¾ C. unsweetened vanilla almond milk

¼ C. avocado oil

1 tsp. vanilla extract

¼ C. allulose granular sugar substitute

2 tsp. baking powder

Pinch of salt

Cooking spray

toppings (optional)

Butter

Sugar free pancake syrup

Berries

DIRECTIONS

1. To a blender, add wet ingredients. Blend until creamy. Add remaining ingredients and blend to mix.

2. Spray a standard size microwave-safe coffee mug and add 3 heaping tablespoons pancake batter. Microwave on high 1 minute.

3. Turn mug pancake out onto a plate and dress with desired toppings, or simply place toppings on top of pancake and eat from the mug.

janeva's tips

Batter makes approximately 12 mug pancakes. For a delicious topping (shown in photo), blend ½ C. sugar free maple syrup, 4 hulled strawberries and 4 fresh raspberries with a stick blender and drizzle over the top.

NET CARBS 1g - per serving (2 pancakes, no toppings)				
calories	fat	protein	carbs	fiber
141	13g	4g	5g	4g

Nutter Butter Waffles

SERVINGS: 4

The internet is bombarded with low carb waffle recipes, and I've probably tried every single one of them. I have not found one that I truly loved until creating this one. It's light, fluffy, and not eggy! This recipe couldn't be simpler; just toss all ingredients into a blender, give them a whirl, and pour into a hot waffle iron for a quick breakfast. I like to make these in batches and freeze for later meals — cool and wrap tightly in plastic wrap, thaw and toast lightly in a toaster to eat.

For an extra special treat, try serving these waffles warmed with a pat of Cinnamon Sunrise Butter, pg. 133 — no syrup needed!

INGREDIENTS

4 eggs

½ C. almond or peanut butter

1 T. Splenda®, granular

½ tsp. baking powder

Pinch sea salt

2 T. melted butter

Cooking spray

DIRECTIONS

1. Preheat waffle iron.

2. Place all ingredients in a blender, food processor or beat with electric mixer until blended. Batter will be very thin.

3. Spray waffle iron, fill waffle iron ¾ full. Bake according to manufacturer directions approximately 1 ½ minutes or until light golden brown.

janeva's tips

Entire recipe makes approximately 8 standard size waffles.

NET CARBS 2g - per serving				
calories	fat	protein	carbs	fiber
302	27g	13g	6g	4g

Rustic Rolls

SERVINGS: 6

I cannot eat mediocre bread. These rolls are fantastic — very wheat-like and rustic — delicious served warmed with salted butter. Better yet, try them spread with sweet or savory flavored compound butters, pg. 132.

INGREDIENTS

1 C. blanched almond flour

¼ C. ground flax seed meal

1 ½ tsp. baking powder

¼ tsp. garlic powder

1 C. shredded mozzarella cheese

1 oz. cream cheese, softened

1 egg, lightly beaten

DIRECTIONS

1. Preheat oven to 350 degrees.
2. To a medium bowl, add dry ingredients; stir to mix well. Set aside.
3. To a microwave proof bowl, add cream cheese and mozzarella cheese. Microwave on high 1 minute. Stir until smooth.
4. Slowly add beaten egg to cheese mixture mixing with a fork until blended.
5. Add dry ingredients to cheese mixture; mix until blended.
6. Line a baking sheet with parchment paper.
7. Scoop batter with a standard size ice cream scoop making 6 rolls.
8. Bake 13-15 minutes or until lightly browned.

NET CARBS 1g - per serving				
calories	fat	protein	carbs	fiber
85	8g	4g	3g	2g

Sausage & Cheddar Breakfast Biscuit

SERVINGS: 6

This is one of my favorite breakfast treats when guests stay with us for the weekend or when I'm just in the mood to indulge a bit. I like to make these in batches and freeze for those occasions. The biscuits are incredible when warmed and topped with salted butter or sliced and sandwiched with a fried or scrambled egg.

INGREDIENTS

2 C. blanched almond flour

½ C. coconut flour

2 tsp. baking powder

½ tsp. onion powder

¼ tsp. salt

2 large eggs

2 T. sour cream

2 T. heavy whipping cream

¾ C. sausage crumbles, cooked (I use Jimmy Dean®)

¾ C. shredded sharp cheddar cheese, divided

DIRECTIONS

1. Preheat oven to 325 degrees.
2. To a large mixing bowl, add almond flour, coconut flour, baking powder, onion powder and salt. Stir to mix.
3. To the flour mixture, add eggs, sour cream and heavy whipping cream. Stir to mix.
4. Fold sausage crumbles and ½ C. cheese into batter.
5. On a parchment lined baking sheet, shape the batter into a 6" x 8" inch rectangle. Cut into 6 even squares.
6. Using a spatula, carefully lift and place biscuits at least one inch apart.
7. Sprinkle biscuits with remaining ¼ C. cheese, and bake 24 - 26 minutes.
8. Transfer biscuits to cooling rack and cool.

janeva's tips

Most low-carb baked goods taste dry when hot out of the oven; these biscuits are not the exception. Let cool completely before eating or reheating – they will moisten as they cool. To heat and eat, place in the microwave oven for 5-8 seconds on high.

NET CARBS 6g - per serving				
calories	fat	protein	carbs	fiber
441	36g	17g	13g	7g

Baked
Scotch Eggs

SERVINGS: 4

These eggs are my go-to for a filling and high protein snack. They're perfect for eating hot or cold and are portable to take on the road too. As an option, mix a little hot sauce into some mayonnaise and drizzle on eggs.

INGREDIENTS

4 hard boiled large eggs

12 oz. bulk pork sausage (I use Jimmy Dean®)

DIRECTIONS

1. Preheat oven to 375 degrees.
2. Divide sausage into 4 equal amounts and pat into 4 large patties.
3. Place egg into center of each patty. Using hands, wrap patty up evenly around egg and seal.
4. Line a baking sheet with parchment paper and place eggs on sheet.
5. Bake 35 minutes or until deep golden brown and done.
6. Eat hot or cold; keep refrigerated if storing. May serve sliced or in wedges drizzled with mayonnaise spiked with hot sauce or eat plain.

NET CARBS 1g - per serving				
calories	fat	protein	carbs	fiber
340	28g	21g	1g	0g

Breakfast Burrito

SERVINGS: 1

I always stock the ingredients in my fridge for this easy breakfast. Delicious served with the Mexican inspired toppings!

INGREDIENTS

burrito

2 large eggs

¼ tsp. Taco Seasoning, pg. 128

1 T. shredded cheddar or pepper jack cheese

1 ready-made low carb tortilla wrap (see tip)

toppings (optional)

Shredded cheddar cheese

Pico de Gallo salsa, pg. 123

Easy Homestyle Salsa, pg. 121

Sliced avocado

Mexican crema or sour cream

Chopped black olives

Chopped fresh cilantro

DIRECTIONS

1. To a microwave safe coffee mug, add eggs, taco seasoning and shredded cheese. Whisk with a fork until eggs are lightly beaten.

2. Microwave on high 90 seconds, mixing half way through cooking time

3. Line the egg mixture down the center of the tortilla wrap; top with desired toppings.

4. Wrap into a burrito to serve.

janeva's tips

Ready-made low carb brand tortilla wraps should be 6 net grams or less to be considered low carb. There are several brands available and are easily found at your local grocers.

NET CARBS 7g				
calories	fat	protein	carbs	fiber
277	14g	18g	7g	0g

Eggs in Purgatory

SERVINGS: 6

These eggs are baked in a fiery red sauce on the stove top. It is unclear where the origin of the name came from; however, it could mean that 'purgatory' refers to the bubbling red tomato sauce or the fire of the red pepper flakes – or maybe both? Either way, this dish uses simple pantry staples and makes for an excellent brunch, lunch or light dinner.

INGREDIENTS

2 T. olive oil

½ tsp. minced garlic

28 oz. can crushed tomatoes

Pinch of Italian seasoning

¼ tsp. red pepper flakes or more, to taste (depending on level of heat desired)

½ tsp. salt

¼ tsp. black pepper

2 T. shredded parmesan cheese

1 T. butter

6 large eggs

Chopped fresh cilantro or parsley, to taste (for garnish)

DIRECTIONS

1. In a large frying pan, heat olive oil over medium heat.

2. Add garlic and stir 30-40 seconds until edges are light golden brown. (Refrain from over cooking or it will become bitter.)

3. Add tomatoes, Italian seasoning, red pepper flakes, salt and pepper. Lower heat to medium low; cover. Cook 20 minutes.

4. Stir parmesan and butter into tomato mixture and place 6 divots in the sauce using the back of a soup ladle or spoon. Crack an egg into each divot.

5. Cover and cook for 3-4 minutes for cooked whites and a runny yolk.

6. Serve topped with fresh chopped cilantro and/or parsley and season with additional black pepper.

janeva's tips

I recommend serving with a good toasted low carb bread for sopping up the purgatory sauce.

NET CARBS 7g - per serving				
calories	fat	protein	carbs	fiber
178	12g	9g	10g	3g

French Kiss Quiche

SERVINGS: 6

If you're looking for that perfect brunch idea for family and/or guests, give this recipe a try. This is an easy but elegant and decadent tasting quiche that will transport you to France!

INGREDIENTS

5 large eggs, lightly beaten

1 C. heavy whipping cream

½ tsp. black pepper

¼ tsp. salt

2 pinches ground nutmeg

¾ C. shredded gouda cheese

¾ C. shredded parmesan cheese

4 slices bacon

2 C. sliced leeks

½ tsp. minced garlic

Cooking spray

DIRECTIONS

1. Preheat oven to 375 degrees.
2. In a medium bowl, combine eggs, cream, pepper, salt and nutmeg; whisk to mix. Set aside.
3. Combine cheeses in a small bowl; set aside.
4. In a medium frying pan, cook bacon on medium/medium high heat until browned and crispy. Drain bacon on a paper towel and crumble. Keep bacon drippings in pan.
5. Heat bacon drippings until hot over medium heat. Add leeks and saute just until light golden brown. Add garlic and stir fry an additional 30 seconds. Remove leeks from pan and set aside.
6. In a sprayed 9" pie plate, evenly spread ½ the cheese mixture. Sprinkle leeks and bacon to cover cheese.
7. Give the egg mixture a few more whisks and pour into pie plate; evenly sprinkle with remaining ½ of cheese mixture.
8. Bake 40 minutes or until center is set. Let stand 5 minutes before serving

NET CARBS 6g - per serving				
calories	fat	protein	carbs	fiber
348	29g	16g	7g	1g

Frico Taco

SERVINGS: 1

Frico = crispy cooked cheese. The frico serves as a taco style vessel for the eggs. This has quickly become a favorite breakfast in our house. We often serve Frico Tacos to our overnight guests always resulting in rave reviews!

INGREDIENTS

2 large eggs

¼ C. shredded parmesan cheese

¼ C. shredded gouda or mozzarella cheese

Salt and pepper, to taste

DIRECTIONS

1. To a cold, small frying pan add shredded cheeses and pat down to distribute evenly; place pan on the stove top and turn burner to medium/medium high heat. Cook 2 ½ minutes or until edges of cheese just start to lightly brown.

2. Crack eggs onto one side of cheese frico; lightly season with salt and pepper and cover. Reduce heat to medium/medium low. Cook 2 ½ minutes, or until egg whites are very lightly cooked over yolks. (The egg will continue to cook during cooling time.)

3. Using a spatula, fold frico over like a taco; place on a cooling rack to cool 2 ½ minutes,

janeva's tips

As an option, additional ingredients such as cooked bacon or sausage crumbles, chopped tomatoes and/or green onion may be added to the taco before folding in half. Nutrition info will change based on cheese brand and type.

NET CARBS 1g - per serving				
calories	fat	protein	carbs	fiber
291	21g	25g	1g	0g

Naked Burrito Frittata

SERVINGS: 4

This dish takes on the flavors of a stuffed burrito without the tortilla wrap – hence, naked! A perfect dish for any meal from breakfast to dinner. Packed with flavor, this frittata will satiate your appetite for hours.

INGREDIENTS

frittata

8 oz. lean ground beef (or chicken or turkey)

1 T. taco seasoning

10 oz. can mild diced tomatoes and green chiles (I use Rotel®)*

5 large eggs

1 T. heavy cream

½ C. shredded Mexican blend cheese or sharp cheddar

1 T. fresh chopped cilantro

Cooking spray

toppings (optional)

Avocado slices

Mexican crema or sour cream

Pico de Gallo, pg. 123

Easy Homestyle Salsa, pg. 121

Chopped green onion

Chopped fresh cilantro

DIRECTIONS

1. Preheat oven to 400 degrees.

2. Heat a medium frying pan over medium/medium high heat, add ground beef and sprinkle in taco seasoning; brown and drain any fat.

3. Spread ground beef evenly in a sprayed 9" glass pie pan.

4. Drain canned tomatoes and chiles and spread evenly over ground beef.

5. Whisk heavy cream and eggs until lightly beaten; stir in cheese and pour over the meat mixture. Sprinkle with cilantro.

6. Bake 25 minutes or just until edge of casserole is set and middle slightly jiggles; it will continue to bake out of oven. Do not over bake, or eggs will go from tender to tough and dry.

7. Cut in wedges and serve with toppings, as desired.

janeva's tips

*If a can of diced tomatoes and green chiles is not available at your grocer, you may use 3/4 C. canned diced tomatoes (drained) and 1/4 C. canned diced green chiles (drained).

NET CARBS 4g - per serving				
calories	fat	protein	carbs	fiber
232	14g	20g	5g	1g

One-Pan
Garden Eggs

SERVINGS: 2

Egg dishes can become ho-hum rather quickly but this recipe using garden fresh squash and tomatoes brightens the dish and tastes divine with sunny-side-up eggs. Breaking the yolk into these caramelized veggies makes for a deliciously decadent but healthy breakfast; however, this egg dish is also wonderful served for any meal of the day!

INGREDIENTS

1 T. olive oil

1 medium zucchini (unpeeled), cut in bite size chunks

1 medium yellow summer squash (unpeeled), cut in bite size chunks

Garlic powder, to taste

1 C. grape or baby heirloom tomatoes, halved

4 large eggs

Salt and pepper, to taste

2 T. water

2 T. shredded parmesan cheese

Chopped fresh basil, optional

DIRECTIONS

1. To a large skillet, heat olive oil over medium heat. Add zucchini and summer squash; sprinkle with garlic powder (I lightly sprinkle and sweep over the pan 2x with the garlic powder.) Cook 5-8 minutes, stirring occasionally, until squash is lightly browned and caramelized.

2. Add tomatoes and cook 2 minutes; gently stir during cooking.

3. Clear 4 open spots in the skillet, and crack eggs into those spots. Season dish with salt and pepper. Add water to skillet and cover. Cook 2-3 minutes or until eggs whites are lightly cooked over egg yolks, leaving the yolks runny.

4. Sprinkle with parmesan cheese; top with chopped basil before serving, if desired.

NET CARBS 6g - per serving				
calories	fat	protein	carbs	fiber
266	18g	17g	9g	3g

Sausage & Egg
Toad in the Hole

SERVINGS: 1

This throwback recipe is inspired by one of my favorite breakfasts from childhood. I can still picture myself in my long floral pajamas sitting at the kitchen table with my siblings in our family's turquoise painted 1960's kitchen, watching Mom make this breakfast for us. Instead of using bread surrounding the 'toad (egg) in the hole', this version uses sausage – not only making it low carb but tasty!

INGREDIENTS

3 oz. bulk pork or turkey sausage (I use Jimmy Dean®)

1 large egg

Salt and pepper, to taste

1 T. water

Easy Homestyle Salsa, pg. 121 (to taste)

DIRECTIONS

1. Roll sausage into an 8" log; form into a circle (like a donut), and pinch ends together. Using the palm of your hand, press down to make a patty with a hole in the center. (Center hole should be about 2" in diameter – doesn't have to be perfectly shaped.)

2. Heat a skillet over medium/medium high heat; add sausage patty. Cook approximately 3-4 minutes or until browned; flip.

3. Crack egg into sausage patty hole; season with salt and pepper. Add water to pan and cover; cook 3-4 minutes or until egg reaches desired doneness and sausage is cooked through.

4. Top with salsa and serve.

janeva's tips

Delicious served with fresh avocado slices on the side. Easily double or triple (or more) the recipe for more servings. To make this dish lower in calories and fat, use turkey sausage in place of pork sausage; adjust nutrition info.

NET CARBS 3g - per serving using pork sausage				
calories	fat	protein	carbs	fiber
414	30g	14g	3g	0g

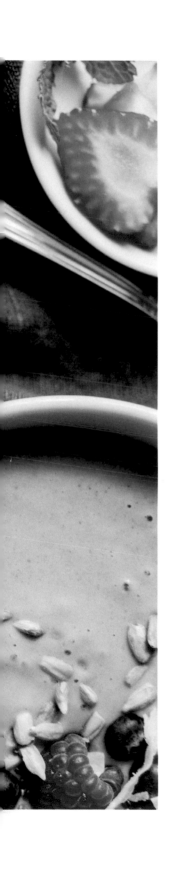

Beverages & Smoothies

contents

Cafe Mocha Protein Smoothie

SERVINGS: 1

Coffee mixed into store-bought prepared protein shakes and poured over ice was a staple breakfast for me especially when I was short on time and wanted something to make and take on-the-go. After realizing the actual costs of the protein shakes are not always budget friendly, I created this version that I find even more delicious and satisfying and less than ½ the cost of store-bought protein shakes. Very quick and easy to make in my bullet blender; I just mix it up, twist the drinking top onto the bullet cup and off I go!

INGREDIENTS

6 oz. cold brewed coffee

3 oz. unsweetened vanilla cashew or almond milk

3 oz. canned unsweetened coconut milk (I use Thai Kitchens®)

1 scoop chocolate whey protein powder

1 tsp. unsweetened cocoa powder

A few drops liquid stevia sweetener, or to taste

1 C. ice

DIRECTIONS

1. Place all ingredients in a blender. Blend on high until smooth and creamy.

janeva's tips

Canned coconut milk will separate in the can. Whisk the coconut milk until creamy before measuring and using in this recipe. Store leftovers in fridge in an airtight plastic container.

NET CARBS 4g - per serving				
calories	fat	protein	carbs	fiber
202	8g	30g	4g	0g

Hot Chocolate

SERVINGS: 6
(¾ C. servings)

I thought hot chocolate might be out of the question for a low carb lifestyle due to the high carbs in dairy milk — but I quickly discovered almond or cashew milk could easily be substituted in its' place. I found that much of the flavor of hot chocolate was coming from heated milk when all I wanted was a rich chocolate flavor. The nut milks add a slight nuttiness to the drink — and that adds to the richness. This hot chocolate is incredibly good and a perfect treat for a cold weather day.

INGREDIENTS

½ C. allulose granular sugar substitute

¼ C. unsweetened cocoa powder

Dash of salt

1/3 C. hot water

3 C. unsweetened plain almond milk

1 C. heavy whipping cream

½ tsp. vanilla extract

DIRECTIONS

1. Mix allulose, cocoa powder and salt in a medium saucepan. Stir in water, and heat to boiling over medium/medium high heat. Reduce heat to medium and cook 2 minutes, stirring constantly.

2. Add almond milk and heavy cream; heat 3 minutes, stirring constantly. Do not boil.

3. Remove from heat and stir in vanilla extract. Serve hot.

NET CARBS 2g - per serving				
calories	fat	protein	carbs	fiber
169	16g	2g	4g	2g

Mean Green Smoothie Bowl

SERVINGS: 1

This super-food breakfast makes me feel energized for the day — and there are days I want to eat my breakfast rather than drink it. Out with the old-school oatmeal and in with the new-school smoothie bowl; this is a delicious alternative with a nutty, maple flavor!

INGREDIENTS

smoothie bowl

½ avocado

1 C. unsweetened vanilla almond or cashew milk

1 C. fresh spinach

1 C. ice

1 T. sugar free maple syrup

1 T. almond butter

toppings (optional)

Fresh berries

Unsweetened coconut flakes

Hemp hearts

Chia seeds

Chopped walnuts or pecans

Slivered almonds

Sunflower seeds

DIRECTIONS

1. Place all smoothie bowl ingredients in a blender; blend on high until smooth and creamy.

2. Pour smoothie into bowl and top with desired toppings — eat with spoon!

NET CARBS 5g - per serving, no toppings				
calories	fat	protein	carbs	fiber
264	22g	6g	13g	8g

Peanut Butter Cup Smoothie

SERVINGS: 1

The healthy version of a childhood favorite.

INGREDIENTS

1 C. unsweetened vanilla cashew or almond milk

½ avocado

2 T. creamy natural peanut butter (no added sugar)

1 T. unsweetened cocoa powder

A few drops liquid stevia sweetener, or to taste

1 C. ice

janeva's tips

The peanut butter cups shown in the picture are sugar free and made by Russel Stover®.

DIRECTIONS

1. Place all ingredients in a blender. Blend on high until smooth and creamy.

NET CARBS 9g - per serving				
calories	fat	protein	carbs	fiber
334	20g	9g	18g	9g

Strawberries 'n Cream Protein Smoothie

SERVINGS: 2

Waking up to this rich and creamy strawberry smoothie makes it worth getting out of bed. I like to make smoothies in batches and freeze individual portions in freezer bags. When needing a quick breakfast, just take a portioned bag out, and let it thaw about 15 minutes. Add to the blender and give it a quick whirl until smooth and creamy – so easy!

INGREDIENTS

¾ c. frozen strawberries

1 scoop vanilla whey protein powder

½ C. canned unsweetened coconut milk (I use Thai Kitchens®)

½ C. unsweetened vanilla almond milk

½ C. plain Greek yogurt, unsweetened

1 T. chia seeds

A few drops liquid stevia sweetener, or to taste

1 C. ice

DIRECTIONS

1. Add all ingredients to a blender. Blend on high until creamy and smooth.

janeva's tips

Canned coconut milk will separate in the can. Whisk the coconut milk until creamy before measuring and using in this recipe. Store leftovers in fridge in an airtight plastic container. The chia seeds are optional, but I keep some on hand as they are a good source of fiber and easily added to smoothies. Nutrition information will vary based on the whey protein brand used in the smoothie.

NET CARBS 8g - per serving				
calories	fat	protein	carbs	fiber
209	12g	13g	12g	4g

Triple Berry Smoothie

SERVINGS: 1

The natural sweetness of the berries combined with the tang of the yogurt and the creaminess of the whipping cream make this smoothie spectacular. Recently, I went to an early morning association meeting and brought this smoothie with me, in a clear bullet cup, for breakfast. The group couldn't keep their eyes off it, and nearly everyone wanted to know where I purchased it because it looks so vibrant and beautiful. When they learned that it was made in a few minutes at home, they requested the recipe without even tasting it – it definitely tastes just as good as it looks!

INGREDIENTS

¾ C. assorted frozen berries (such as blackberries, raspberries and blueberries)

¾ C. unsweetened vanilla almond milk

2 T. heavy whipping cream

½ C. Greek or regular vanilla yogurt (low sugar)

A few drops of liquid Stevia, or to taste (optional)

janeva's tips

When choosing a yogurt, be sure to read the nutrition label. There are can be hidden sugars in many yogurt brands. The nutrition information is based on using Two Good® yogurt which has quickly become a favorite of mine. This smoothie makes a great breakfast treat to enjoy occasionally due to the higher carbs from the fruit; however, you may still work it nicely into a low carb menu for the day.

DIRECTIONS

1. Place all ingredients in a blender, and blend on high until smooth and creamy. Taste and adjust sweetener, if necessary.

NET CARBS 14g - per serving				
calories	fat	protein	carbs	fiber
239	14g	11g	17g	3g

low carb libations

There are several alcohols that are low in carbs. While cocktails don't offer much nutrition, they are allowed in a low carb lifestyle. An alcoholic beverage is manageable when planned into your menu for the week or month or whatever fits your lifestyle. So, when the social hour strikes, know that you have a few great options.

LOW CARB WINE   per 5 oz. serving

Dry white wines tend to have 1-2 carbs per 5 oz. serving. Other wine selections (such as red wines) will average approximately 4 carbs per 5 oz serving. Listed are some good options for lower carb wines but the carbs will vary by brand:

Cabernet Sauvignon

Pinot Noir

Chardonnay

Sauvignon Blanc

Chablis

Zinfandel

LOW CARB ALCOHOL   per 1 oz. serving

Club soda, diet tonic or plain water work well as sugar free mixers. Add a wedge of lemon or lime to provide a refreshing twist.

Rum	0 g carbs
Tequila	0 g carbs
Vodka	0 g carbs
Gin	0 g carbs
Whiskey (Bourbon, Rye, Scotch)	0.02 g carbs
Cognac & Brandy	0 g carbs

LOW CARB BEER   per 12 oz. serving

There are several beers on the market that won't derail your low carb efforts. To be considered low carb, opt for brands that are 2-4 g carbohydrates per 12 ounces beer.

Hop, Skip & Go Naked

SERVINGS: 2

Also known as the Porchcrawler in some regions, the Hop, Skip and Go Naked version is popular in the Midwest. Always containing beer, vodka or gin and a citrus addition, this drink packs a carbonated punch with a fruity taste. A perfect libation for sipping during hot weather -- super refreshing too!

INGREDIENTS

12 oz. low-carb beer (I use Michelob® Ultra)

2 oz. vodka

¼ tsp. Mio® lemonade liquid water enhancer

1 T. cold water

Ice cubes

DIRECTIONS

1. Fill 2 pint size glasses with ice cubes.

2. Combine liquid ingredients, and pour over ice.

NET CARBS 1.6g - per serving				
calories	fat	protein	carbs	fiber
110	0g	1g	1.6g	0g

Irish Cream Liqueur

SERVINGS: 14
(2 oz. serving size)

Irish cream liqueur is always a holiday favorite or served any time as an after-dinner drink. Excellent served on the rocks or enjoyed in a hot coffee. This low carb version for Irish cream liqueur is divine. Bailey? Who's Bailey?

INGREDIENTS

1 C. Irish whiskey (I use Jameson®)

2 C. heavy whipping cream

¼ C. erythritol confectioners sugar (I use Swerve®)

2 tsp. unsweetened cocoa powder

1 tsp. instant espresso granules

1 tsp. pure vanilla extract

1 tsp. pure almond extract

DIRECTIONS

1. Place all ingredients in a blender. Pulse to mix until combined.

2. Store in the fridge in a covered container for up to 1 month.

janeva's tips

Recipe makes approximately 3 ½ C.

NET CARBS 1g - per serving				
calories	fat	protein	carbs	fiber
160	13g	1g	1g	0g

Lemon Lime Vodka Soda

SERVINGS: 2

Cool and crisp with a hint of citrus – this cocktail is perfect for a bar stop or made at home for happy hour.

INGREDIENTS

1 ½ oz. (1 shot) vodka

3 oz. club soda

2 lemon wedges

2 lime wedges

Ice cubes

DIRECTIONS

1. Fill two lowball glasses with ice.

2. Equally pour vodka and soda over ice.

3. Squeeze a lemon and lime wedge into each drink; submerge wedges into glass and stir.

NET CARBS 1g - per serving				
calories	fat	protein	carbs	fiber
97	0g	0g	1g	0g

Twisted Palmer

SERVINGS: 1

Golfer Arnold Palmer's favorite drink was a mixture of ½ lemonade and ½ sweet tea over ice. It is appropriately called an 'Arnold Palmer'. The Twisted Palmer is spiked with vodka – hence the twist. This drink is refreshing and easy to sip on a warm day – but a cold day works too!

INGREDIENTS

1 ½ oz. (1 shot) vodka

3 oz. sugar free iced tea, prepared (I use Mio®)

3 oz. sugar free lemonade, prepared (I use Mio®)

Lemon wedge

Ice

DIRECTIONS

1. Fill a high ball glass with ice. Pour vodka, iced tea and lemonade into glass, and stir. Squeeze lemon wedge into drink and submerge.

janeva's tips

Calories will vary based on brand of vodka used in recipe — 80 proof vodkas are lowest in calorie at approximately 64 calories for 1 ounce.

NET CARBS 0g - per serving				
calories	fat	protein	carbs	fiber
96	0g	0g	0g	0g

Wine Spritzer

SERVINGS: 1

Why would you want to ruin a perfectly good glass of white wine by adding something to it? That was my thought before I tried a wine spritzer. The bubbly club soda elevates the wine by offering a sparkling, crisp, and refreshing taste. Visually it 'stretches' out the volume for each glass and that's appealing as well!

INGREDIENTS

6 oz. red or dry white wine, chilled

2 oz. cold club soda

Ice, optional

Fresh raspberry, lemon rind, or mint sprig for garnish (optional)

DIRECTIONS

1. Fill an oversized wine glass with the wine. Top with club soda and serve ice cold (or over ice). Garnish, if desired.

janeva's tips

To be sure the spritzer is well chilled, I often put the wine bottle in the freezer for about 1 hour and the club soda for about 20 minutes – then make the spritzer. If this is not an option, the spritzer may be served over ice.   Nutrition info will vary based on brand and type of wine used in recipe.

NET CARBS 1.6g - per serving				
calories	fat	protein	carbs	fiber
110	0g	1g	1.6g	0g

"some of my favorite happy hour snacks are stuffed olives, nuts and gourmet cheeses."

Salads
& Soups

contents

Avocado Shrimp Ceviche

SERVINGS: 4

My first experience eating ceviche was in Mexico on an island while on vacation, and I fell in love with the freshness and flavor of this dish. I like to serve the ceviche on cucumber slices, low carb crackers or low carb tortilla chips as an appetizer. No judgment if you just want to spoon it straight into your mouth!

INGREDIENTS

1 lb. medium shrimp, thawed (cooked, deveined, tails off)

1 ½ C. diced Roma tomatoes

1 C. cubed avocado

1 C. diced cucumber (peeled and pulp removed*)

¼ C. chopped green onion

¼ C. chopped fresh cilantro

Juice of 1 lime

1 T. lemon juice

½ C. diced red or yellow onion

1 ½ tsp. minced jalapeno pepper (seeds and membrane removed)

Salt & pepper, to taste

DIRECTIONS

1. Cut the cooked shrimp in small chunks; place in a medium sized bowl.

2. Add remaining ingredients and gently mix together.

3. Store ceviche covered in fridge until ready for use

janeva's tips

*To remove pulp in cucumber, cut in half lengthwise and run a spoon down the center; discard pulp.

NET CARBS 7g - per serving				
calories	fat	protein	carbs	fiber
166	6g	30g	12g	5g

Blackened Chicken Salad

SERVINGS: 2

Inspired by a salad offered at one of my favorite local restaurants, this revised version has become my all-time favorite salad. It makes a great lunch or dinner that is light but filling and satisfying. I can't rave about it enough.

INGREDIENTS

2 chicken breasts (boneless and skinless)

Cajun or Creole seasoning, to taste

1 T. olive oil

1 bunch romaine lettuce, chopped

¼ C. crumbled feta cheese

¼ C. finely shredded cheddar cheese

2 Roma tomatoes, chopped

2 T. chopped green onion

4 strips cooked bacon, crumbled

¼ C. ranch dressing

DIRECTIONS

1. Place chicken breasts in a large zip plastic bag. Pound to approximately ½" thickness with a meat mallet. Transfer to a plate and sprinkle both sides with seasoning.

2. Heat oil in a large frying pan over medium/medium high heat; place chicken breasts in pan and cook 3 minutes on each side. Remove and let rest on a clean plate while prepping salad.

3. In a large mixing bowl, add all salad ingredients (except chicken); toss and plate.

4. Drizzle with desired amount of dressing to your liking; cut chicken breasts in slices and lay on top of salad(s).

janeva's tips

Bottled or homemade ranch dressing may be used; select one lower in carbs. Dressing is not included in nutrition info below due to the variation in brands. Check nutrition label and add dressing nutrition info accordingly.

NET CARBS 6g - per serving, no dressing				
calories	fat	protein	carbs	fiber
378	27g	39g	9g	3g

Caprese
Salad

SERVINGS: 8

In my many travels to Italy, most of our dinners started with this salad which seems to be a staple countrywide. Could it have something to do with the green, white and red colors representing their flag? Nonetheless, it's a light and fresh salad that works for lunch, a side at dinner, or even a snack.

INGREDIENTS

1 lb. mozzarella pearls

2 C. (1 pint) cherry or baby heirloom tomatoes, halved

¼ C. balsamic vinegar

¼ C. extra virgin olive oil

2 – 3 T. chopped fresh basil

Salt and pepper, to taste

DIRECTIONS

1. Add mozzarella and tomatoes to a medium bowl; set aside.

2. In a small bowl, combine vinegar, olive oil and basil, and whisk with a fork. Pour over tomato mixture, and season with salt and pepper. Cover and marinate in fridge 30 minutes; stir midway through.

3. Sprinkle with additional fresh basil, if desired.

janeva's tips

To quickly and easily cut tomatoes, choose two plastic container lids that are the same size, and place tomatoes in between lids on a flat work surface. Gently pressing down on the top lid with the palm of one hand (with fingers out of the way), use the other hand to cut horizontally through the center of the tomatoes with a long sharp knife from one edge to the other. You may do this in batches depending on the size of the lids and length of the knife.

NET CARBS 3g - per serving				
calories	fat	protein	carbs	fiber
219	17g	10g	4g	1g

Cauliflower Tabouli Salad

SERVINGS: 6

Tabouli, or tabbouleh, is a vegetarian salad comprised mainly of chopped veggies, mint, oil, lemon juice, and typically, bulgar wheat. In this version, cauliflower replaces the bulgar wheat for a fresh and light salad option. While not always typical, some like this salad with feta cheese, an optional ingredient in this recipe. Frozen cauliflower will not work for this dish. To rice fresh cauliflower, see tip below.

INGREDIENTS

salad

2 C. riced cauliflower

¾ C. grape tomatoes, quartered

½ C. chopped cucumber (peeled)

¼ C. chopped green onion

¼ C. chopped fresh parsley

2 T. chopped fresh mint

Salt and pepper, to taste

½ C. crumbled feta cheese (optional)

dressing

1/3 C. lemon juice

3 T. olive oil

1 T. soy sauce

DIRECTIONS

1. In a large bowl, gently toss salad ingredients. Set aside.

2. In a medium bowl, whisk together the dressing ingredients.

3. Just before serving, pour dressing over cauliflower mixture and fold to coat salad.

4. Cover and refrigerate any leftovers.

janeva's tips

To rice fresh cauliflower, you may grate cauliflower florets on the largest hole of a cheese grater, or place in a food processor and pulse the florets to rice size bits. I prefer the latter, making prep a cinch.

NET CARBS 4g - per serving				
calories	fat	protein	carbs	fiber
120	10g	4g	6g	2g

Cobb Salad Wrap

SERVINGS: 1

All of these ingredients are simple enough to find at any grocery store and easy enough to keep stored in the refrigerator for a quick meal. Even the hard-boiled eggs can be purchased pre-cooked so assembly is a cinch. It's like eating a salad with your bare hands and is easy to take on-the-go.

INGREDIENTS

1 large butter lettuce leaf

2 slices deli ham

2 slices deli smoked turkey

2 tsp. mayonnaise

1 T. crumbled blue cheese

1 slice tomato

1 hard-boiled egg, sliced

Salt & pepper, to taste

DIRECTIONS

1. Lay lettuce leaf flat and arrange ham and turkey on entire leaf.

2. Arrange remaining ingredients over one half. Fold the other half over filling and eat like a taco or roll into a wrap.

janeva's tips

Delicious served with sliced avocado sprinkled with 'Everything' bagel seasoning, found in most grocery stores, Costco, or Trader Joe's.

NET CARBS 7g - per serving				
calories	fat	protein	carbs	fiber
299	18g	28g	7g	0g

Creamy Ranch Cucumber & Radish Salad

SERVINGS: 4

This salad is light and refreshing and pairs well with smoky meats grilled outdoors. It also works as a light lunch idea or side to any meal. Truth be told I am not a huge fan of radishes, but I adore the combination of flavors and crispy crunch in this recipe – definitely worth giving this one a try!

INGREDIENTS

1 English cucumber, sliced thin (unpeeled)

10 radishes, sliced thin (unpeeled, discard ends)

2 green onions, chopped

¾ C. sour cream

1 T. Hidden Valley® ranch seasoning mix (dry)

¼ tsp. salt, or to taste

1/8 tsp. black pepper, or to taste

Chopped fresh chives or dill, to taste (for topping)

DIRECTIONS

1. To a large bowl, add cucumber, radishes and green onion. Cover and refrigerate.

2. In a medium bowl, mix together the remaining ingredients. Cover and refrigerate.

3. Just before serving, fold sour cream mixture into salad veggies until combined. Transfer to a serving dish.

4. Sprinkle with fresh herbs. Serve chilled.

janeva's tips

After sour cream mixture is combined with the salad veggies, the sour cream and cucumbers will begin to leach moisture. If storing leftovers in fridge and just before serving, pour or drain the liquid and fold before serving. As an option, and to brighten the salad, mix in a dollop of sour cream and season as necessary.

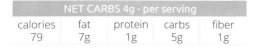

NET CARBS 4g - per serving				
calories	fat	protein	carbs	fiber
79	7g	1g	5g	1g

Grilled Romaine Chicken Caesar Salad

SERVINGS: 2

Grilled romaine lettuce adds a smoky grilled flavor to any salad and elevates this classic Caesar salad. After tasting this recipe version, you may just want to seal it with a 'bellisimo' fingertip kiss!

INGREDIENTS

2 chicken breasts, boneless & skinless

Sea salt, to taste

Black pepper, to taste

2 T. olive or avocado oil, divided

1 whole head of romaine lettuce

¼ C. Caesar dressing, pg. 119

¼ C. shredded parmesan cheese

janeva's tips

Grilled romaine hearts may also be served chopped and tossed in a salad to add tremendous flavor!

DIRECTIONS

1. Place chicken breasts in a large resealable plastic bag. Using a meat mallet, pound chicken breasts evenly to ½" thick. Season both sides with salt and pepper; set aside.

2. Add 1 T. olive oil to a stove top grill pan (or large skillet); heat over medium/medium high heat. Place chicken breasts on pan, and cook each side 3 minutes. Plate, cover, and set aside.

3. Cut romaine head in half from root end to tip and slice off any brown spots on stem end (keeping stems intact.) Remove any loose or bruised outer leaves, revealing the center hearts of the romaine. Brush both sides of romaine hearts with 1 T. olive oil; season lightly with salt and pepper.

4. Heat stove top grill pan (or large skillet) over medium/medium high heat. When pan is hot, place romaine hearts on pan and grill both sides until lightly browned. This only takes a few minutes on each side.

5. Plate grilled romaine hearts cut side up. Top with sliced grilled chicken, drizzle with dressing and sprinkle with cheese. Season with salt and pepper, if desired.

NET CARBS 4g - per serving				
calories	fat	protein	carbs	fiber
553	30g	45g	4g	0g

Janeva's Simple Salad

SERVINGS: 6

Seems like a simple salad? It is! Great tasting food doesn't need to have complex ingredients; it just has to have the right balance of flavors – and this one has just that. The most under seasoned dish is salads, and two of the key ingredients in this salad are the sea salt and coarsely ground black pepper – trust the recipe. During my travels to Argentina, our meals always started with a simple and rustic salad, and so I've created a copycat of this South American staple that is a perfect side to any meal. When I am asked to bring a salad to a gathering, this is one of my favorites and it's always a hit.

INGREDIENTS

8 C. chopped red leaf lettuce or red and green butter lettuce leaves

2 Roma tomatoes

½ medium yellow onion

2 T. mild olive oil

2 T. Heinz® gourmet salad vinegar or apple cider vinegar

¼ tsp. sea salt

1/8 tsp. coarsely ground black pepper (I use McCormick's®)

DIRECTIONS

1. Add lettuce to a large salad bowl; set aside.

2. Thinly slice tomatoes and onion; cut round slices in half. Add to lettuce; gently toss.

3. Just before serving, drizzle olive oil and vinegar over salad. Sprinkle with salt and pepper. Gently toss.

janeva's tips

I highly recommend using the Heinz® salad vinegar vs. the apple cider vinegar. Both are good; however, I find the malt vinegar in the Heinz® brand offers an extra special flavor to this salad. Using the lettuce variety recommended in this recipe is key to this salad; other lettuce varieties will not work as well.

NET CARBS 1g - per serving				
calories	fat	protein	carbs	fiber
56	5g	1g	2g	1g

Jicama Sweet Pepper Slaw

SERVINGS: 4

This salad is often on rotation in my home -- we love it. It's an excellent go-to dish for larger gatherings as well. Don't be surprised at the compliments received, many times over!

INGREDIENTS

2 C. julienned jicama (cut the size of matchsticks)

1 C. julienned bell peppers (red and yellow)

2 T. olive oil

1 T. apple cider vinegar

1 T. maple pancake syrup, sugar free

1 T. minced red onion

½ tsp. garlic powder

¼ tsp. ground cumin

2 T. chopped fresh cilantro

Salt & pepper, to taste

DIRECTIONS

1. Place the julienned jicama and bell pepper in a large bowl; set aside.

2. In a medium bowl, whisk the remaining ingredients until mixed.

3. Pour the dressing over the jicama and bell pepper; toss to coat. Keep refrigerated until use.

janeva's tips

I store this slaw in a large resealable plastic bag in the fridge. That way, it's easy to turn to coat before serving.

NET CARBS 6g - per serving				
calories	fat	protein	carbs	fiber
101	7g	1g	10g	4g

Lynda's Basic Egg Salad

SERVINGS: 3

INGREDIENTS

6 hard-boiled eggs

1/3 C. mayonnaise

1 tsp. yellow mustard

½ tsp. lemon juice

Sea salt, to taste

Black pepper, to taste

DIRECTIONS

1. In a medium bowl, mash eggs with a fork until finely chopped. Add remaining ingredients and stir to mix. Refrigerate until use.

janeva's tips

A pastry cutter works nicely to chop up the eggs; finish mashing with a fork to a finer texture.

NET CARBS 2g - per serving				
calories	fat	protein	carbs	fiber
297	27g	11g	2g	0g

Lynda's Ultimate Egg Salad

SERVINGS: 4

INGREDIENTS

8 hard-boiled eggs

½ C. mayonnaise

1 tsp. yellow mustard

¼ tsp. smoked paprika

1/8 tsp. garlic powder

2 T. chopped green onion

1 T. chopped red onion

½ celery rib, chopped

2 tsp. chopped fresh chives

1 tsp. chopped fresh dill

Salt and pepper, to taste

DIRECTIONS

1. Mash eggs with a fork to desired texture. Set aside.

2. To a medium mixing bowl, add mayonnaise, mustard, paprika, garlic powder. Mix to blend.

3. Add eggs and remaining ingredients to mayonnaise mixture and fold to mix. Taste and season with additional salt and pepper, if necessary.

NET CARBS 2g - per serving				
calories	fat	protein	carbs	fiber
334	30g	13g	2g	0g

My sister asks me to make my egg salad recipe for her birthday every year. I make two different versions which I will share with you here. The first version is basic, the one she enjoys most, which is the reason I put her name on this recipe. When I asked Lynda what was so special about the egg salad, she replied that it is 'so fluffy and balanced in flavor.' The fluffiness comes from mashing the eggs a bit finer than a rough chop.

The second recipe is for the Ultimate Egg Salad and boasts elevated flavor by using fresh herbs, seasonings, and other goodies.

Melon & Pecan Chicken Salad

SERVINGS: 4

I've always enjoyed fruit in a nutty chicken salad; the sweet and savory flavor pleases the palate just perfectly. While grapes are a typical fruit addition to chicken salads, they are very high in carbs -- so I've used my other favorite lower carb fruit in this recipe – cantaloupe! To elevate this old-school classic dish with new-school flavor, try subbing the pecans with Blue Diamond® wasabi and soy almonds. Whoa!

INGREDIENTS

3 C. cooked & diced chicken

½ C. mayonnaise

¼ tsp. sea salt

1/8 tsp. black pepper

2 T. finely diced yellow onion

2 T. diced celery

¼ C. chopped pecans

Butter lettuce leaves, to taste

2 C. cubed cantaloupe

Chopped fresh parsley, to taste (optional)

DIRECTIONS

1. To a medium bowl, add chicken, mayonnaise, salt and pepper. Fold to coat chicken.

2. Add onion, celery and pecans; fold to mix. Refrigerate until ready to use.

3. To serve, plate lettuce leaves and top with cantaloupe. Place a scoop of chicken salad on top. Sprinkle with parsley, if desired.

janeva's tips

Using the meat from the whole roasted deli chickens found in most grocery stores adds so much flavor to this salad; I won't eat it any other way.

NET CARBS 10g - per serving				
calories	fat	protein	carbs	fiber
483	34g	32g	12g	2g

Strawberry Fields Salad

SERVINGS: 2

Fresh field greens topped with strawberries and other goodies make this salad extra tasty – and drizzled with warm bacon dressing puts it out of this world. You may sub the warm bacon dressing with your other favorite dressing such as a low carb poppy seed dressing – but I wouldn't hesitate to add some crumbled bacon if you do!

INGREDIENTS

2 C. fresh spinach leaves, stems removed and loosely packed

2 C. arugula

¼ C. crumbled feta cheese

½ C. thinly sliced red onion

1/3 C. whole pecans

10 strawberries (medium size), quartered

2 T. Warm Bacon Dressing, pg. 130

DIRECTIONS

1. To a large mixing bowl, add spinach and arugula; toss.

2. Top with remaining salad ingredients; drizzle with dressing.

NET CARBS 9g - per serving, no dressing				
calories	fat	protein	carbs	fiber
234	18g	7g	14g	5g

salads & soups

Tequilaberry's Salad

SERVINGS: 6

This recipe was inspired by a salad served at Tequilaberry's restaurant near my home. It was so popular that many people went just for the salad which was prepped and served tableside at every meal. This is a low carb copycat recipe that tastes every bit as delicious; I find this a perfect luncheon salad, since the calories can add up if adding to a dinner meal.

INGREDIENTS

dressing

1 C. mayonnaise

½ C. shredded parmesan cheese

¼ C. allulose granular sugar substitute

2 T. heavy whipping cream

2 T. water

salad

1 lb. bacon, cooked and crumbled

4 C. shredded lettuce

3 C. chopped cauliflower (pearl size)

DIRECTIONS

1. In a medium bowl, whisk all dressing ingredients until combined. Refrigerate at least 1 hour before dressing the salad.

2. In a large bowl, toss salad ingredients. Pour dressing over salad; gently toss until all salad ingredients are dressed.

janeva's tips

To make this salad super easy, I purchase the shredded lettuce and cauliflower pearls already prepped from the grocer. Be sure to use fresh cauliflower, not frozen.

NET CARBS 4g - per serving				
calories	fat	protein	carbs	fiber
446	41g	14g	7g	3g

Thai Peanut Slaw

SERVINGS: 8

This slaw is full of Thai flavor and calls for one carrot. No worries about the carbs, the carrot is divided by eight servings in this recipe resulting in minimal carbs per serving. You may omit the carrot if you don't want to use it; however, it adds great color and even better taste. I think I might be slightly obsessed with this crave-worthy slaw.

INGREDIENTS

slaw

8 C. shredded green cabbage (about ½ large head)

4 C. shredded red cabbage (about ½ small head)

1 carrot, shredded

peanut dressing

¼ C. creamy peanut butter

3 T. sugar free honey or sugar free maple pancake syrup*

2 tsp. minced ginger

1 tsp. minced garlic

1 T. + 2 tsp. soy sauce

2 T. rice vinegar

2 T. lime juice

1 T. + 1 tsp. liquid coconut oil

1 tsp. sesame oil

1/8 tsp. salt

¼ tsp. hot sauce

toppings

½ C. 1/2 C. salted peanuts, halved or chopped (no skins)

¼ C. chopped green onion

DIRECTIONS

1. To a large bowl, add slaw ingredients and toss to mix.

2. In a medium bowl, whisk peanut dressing ingredients until smooth and creamy. Pour over slaw and toss to mix.

3. Before serving, top with peanuts and green onion. Serve chilled.

janeva's tips

*In this recipe, I prefer using sugar free honey rather than sugar free maple syrup. I use Honeytree® brand which can easily be found online and at retailers such as Amazon. After preparing the slaw, refrigerating a few hours before serving is suggested. The cabbage will start to wilt from the dressing making it a better texture for eating.

NET CARBS 9g - per serving				
calories	fat	protein	carbs	fiber
145	10g	5g	13g	4g

Cabbage Roll Soup

SERVINGS: 8
(1 ¾ C. serving size)

This cabbage roll soup has all the flavors of stuffed cabbage rolls but requires far less work! Cabbage and beef are simmered in a rich fire-roasted tomato broth for the ultimate bowl of comfort food.

INGREDIENTS

2 T. butter

2 stalks celery, chopped

½ large yellow onion, chopped

2 lbs. ground beef (85% lean)

2 tsp. salt

1 tsp. black pepper

½ tsp. garlic powder

1 tsp. onion powder

2 – 14 oz. cans fire roasted diced tomatoes (I use Hunt's®), undrained*

15 oz. can tomato sauce

2 tsp. Worcestershire sauce

½ medium head cabbage, chopped

DIRECTIONS

1. Melt butter over medium/medium high heat in a stockpot or Dutch oven. Add celery and onion; stir fry 5 minutes.

2. Add ground beef, salt, pepper, garlic powder and onion powder; brown (do not drain).

3. Add remaining ingredients; stir. Bring soup to a boil. Cover and reduce heat to medium low. Simmer 40 – 45 minutes or until cabbage is soft and tender.

janeva's tips

*I use fire roasted tomatoes to add flavor; however, any flavor such as basil, garlic or plain may be used. If using plain diced tomatoes, season with additional seasonings, to taste (if necessary).   Recipe makes approximately 14 C. soup.

NET CARBS 9g - per serving				
calories	fat	protein	carbs	fiber
281	15g	25g	12g	3g

Cheeseburger Soup

SERVINGS: 8

When you're in the mood for a cheeseburger, this soup hits the spot – and no bun needed! It's decadent and rich and satiates the appetite.

INGREDIENTS

soup

2 lb. lean ground beef (or chicken or turkey)

2 T. dried minced onion

1 tsp. garlic powder

3 C. beef broth

4 tsp. Worcestershire sauce

1 T. Dijon mustard

1 - 10 oz. can diced original or hot tomatoes and green chiles (I use Rotel®)

1 tsp. sea salt

½ tsp. black pepper

1 C. heavy cream

2 C. shredded sharp cheddar cheese

toppings (optional)

8 slices bacon, cooked and chopped

Chopped pickles, to taste

DIRECTIONS

1. To a Dutch oven or stockpot, add ground beef, minced onion and garlic powder. Brown over medium/medium high heat. Drain any fat.

2. Add remaining ingredients except heavy cream and cheese. Bring to a bubble and turn burner to low heat; cover and simmer for 20 minutes.

3. Add cream and cheese. Cover and simmer 20 minutes, stirring occasionally. Uncover and simmer to desired texture -- soup will thicken as it cooks.

4. Top with pickles and bacon just before serving, if desired.

NET CARBS 5g - per serving, no toppings				
calories	fat	protein	carbs	fiber
409	30g	30g	6g	1g

Creamy Tomato Basil Soup

SERVINGS: 6

When my best friend and I were hungry for a good soup, we would head to a casino near her home solely for the creamy tomato basil soup they serve at their restaurant. We tried to get the recipe from the chef, the waitress, the hostess and the management – but no one would oblige – so I set out to make this version of the soup we love so much. I may be partial, but I think they should no—w use this recipe instead! This soup is rich, hearty, and over the top delicious served with crumbled Cheese Crisps sprinkled on top. You'll find the recipe for those on pg. 282.

INGREDIENTS

soup

5 T. salted butter, divided

½ C. chopped yellow onion

1 tsp. minced garlic

1 ½ C. chicken stock

28 oz. can crushed tomatoes

3 fresh basil leaves, stems removed

½ tsp. salt

¼ tsp. black pepper

1 C. heavy whipping cream

toppings (optional)

Cheese Crisps, pg. 282 (crumbled)

Fresh chopped basil

Heavy whipping cream (drizzled)

DIRECTIONS

1. In a large stockpot or Dutch oven, melt 3 T. butter over medium heat. Add onion and cook until onion is translucent (about 5 minutes). Add garlic and cook an additional 30 seconds, stirring constantly.

2. Add chicken stock, tomatoes, basil, salt and pepper and bring to a low boil.

3. Reduce heat to medium low; cover and simmer 20 minutes, stirring occasionally.

4. Remove stockpot from heat. Using an immersion blender, blend soup in the stockpot until smooth. (If you don't have an immersion blender you may blend in a regular blender; however, hot liquids can blow the top off so be sure to hold onto that when blending.)

5. Place stockpot back on medium low heat; stir in heavy cream. Cover and simmer an additional 15 minutes, stirring occasionally. Add remaining 2 T. butter and stir till melted.

6. Serve with toppings, if desired.

janeva's tips

An easy alternative to the homemade Cheese Crisps are the Whisps® parmesan cheese crisps; I purchase them at Costco.

NET CARBS 8g - per serving, no toppings				
calories	fat	protein	carbs	fiber
264	24g	3g	10g	2g

Hot & Sour Soup

SERVINGS: 6

This soup will rival any you will find at a Chinese restaurant. You may surprise yourself at how easy it is to make and how delicious it is to eat. For a heartier soup, I highly recommend adding cooked bite size pieces of chicken or pork (good way to use left overs) to the prepared soup. A deli roasted chicken works well. Spectacular!

INGREDIENTS

8 C. chicken stock

8 oz. thinly sliced shiitake or baby Bella mushrooms, stems discarded

8 oz. can bamboo shoots, drained

¼ C. soy sauce

¼ C. rice vinegar (I use Marukan® brand)

1 ½ tsp. ground ginger

2 tsp. chili garlic sauce

1 T. glucomannan powder (konjac powder)

1 T. water

2 large eggs, lightly beaten

½ C. chopped green onions, divided

1 tsp. toasted sesame oil

Salt and pepper, to taste

Cooked chicken or pork, to taste (optional)

DIRECTIONS

1. To a large stockpot or Dutch oven, add chicken stock, mushrooms, bamboo shoots, soy sauce, rice vinegar, ground ginger and chili garlic sauce. Heat to a low boil and turn down to a simmer over medium/medium low heat.

2. In a small bowl, stir glucomannan powder and water until dissolved. Add to soup and stir about one minute to thicken soup.

3. Continue stirring in a circular motion while drizzling in eggs.

4. Add sesame oil and ¼ C. green onions (and chicken or pork, if using), and heat through.

5. Serve in soup bowls; sprinkle with salt, pepper and remaining ¼ C. green onions for garnish.

janeva's tips

For more heat, add more chili garlic sauce; for a more sour taste, add more rice vinegar. Nutrition info includes soup only. If adding pork or chicken to soup, add to nutrition info.

NET CARBS 1g - per serving				
calories	fat	protein	carbs	fiber
81	3g	6g	5g	4g

Sausage Chili Con Carne
crockpot recipe

SERVINGS: 6

This recipe won first place in a chili cook-off event among friends at a large gathering. The sausage adds rich flavor, the spices lend a smoky flavor and the veggies lend a meaty bite in place of beans. This is a tasty and easy chili recipe the whole family will love.

INGREDIENTS

chili

1 lb. lean ground beef

1 lb. bulk pork sausage (I use Jimmy Dean®)

1 C. diced green bell pepper

6 cloves garlic, minced

2 T. olive oil

½ tsp. salt

¼ tsp. black pepper

3 T. cumin

1 ½ T. chili powder

28 oz. can crushed tomatoes

7 oz. can mild green chiles

1 C. sliced fresh mushrooms

toppings (optional)

Sour cream

Shredded cheddar cheese

Chopped green or yellow onion

DIRECTIONS

1. Heat a large skillet on medium/medium high heat; add ground beef, sausage and garlic; brown. Drain any fat.

2. Add all ingredients to crockpot; stir to mix. Cook on low 6 hours.

3. Top each serving with a dollop of sour cream and sprinkle with cheese and onion, if desired.

janeva's tips

Toppings not included in nutritional info; add if consuming. Ground poultry may be subbed for the beef and pork as a variation of this recipe.

NET CARBS 11g - per serving (no toppings)				
calories	fat	protein	carbs	fiber
432	28g	30g	14g	3g

Zuppa Toscana

SERVINGS: 6
(1 1/3 C. serving size)
Recipe makes 8 C. soup.

This soup is a take on a copycat recipe from a popular Italian restaurant. The soup is typically made with potatoes, but in this recipe radishes take their place. Radishes? No worries, they lose their bitterness and if you didn't know they were radishes, you'd think they were potatoes – incredibly delicious and a must try! I like using hot sausage to give the soup a spicy heat, but regular also gives it a delicious smoky sausage flavor.

INGREDIENTS

1 lb. bulk sausage, regular or hot (I use Jimmy Dean®)

1 tsp. garlic powder

6 slices bacon, chopped in ½" pieces

½ lb. (2 C.) trimmed and quartered radishes

½ large yellow onion, chopped

4 C. chicken stock

2 C. water

4 C. chopped fresh kale (Tuscan or curly)

1 ½ C. heavy whipping cream

DIRECTIONS

1. In a large frying pan over medium heat, brown sausage and garlic powder. Drain and set aside.

2. Place chopped bacon in a stockpot or Dutch oven; brown over medium heat, stirring frequently. Remove from heat; transfer bacon with a slotted spoon to paper towels to drain. Leave 2 T. bacon drippings in pot.

3. Return pot to stove top over medium heat; add radishes and onion. Cook until vegetables just begin to brown (about 10 -12 minutes).

4. Add chicken stock and water. Simmer 15 minutes.

5. Add sausage and kale; simmer 5 minutes.

6. Add heavy cream; simmer 5 minutes, stirring often.

7. Serve hot, sprinkled with bacon.

NET CARBS 7g - per serving				
calories	fat	protein	carbs	fiber
553	49g	19g	9g	2g

Condiments

contents

Avocado Lime Crema

SERVINGS: 12

This fresh and flavorful crema makes a great dip or dressing and is excellent for dipping veggies, spreading on sandwiches, drizzling on tacos or fajitas, topping Mexican dishes, casseroles, eggs and more. To use as a dressing on salads, just add more water until desired consistency. You will want to put this on everything!

INGREDIENTS

2 ripe avocados, peeled and pits removed

½ C. packed fresh cilantro

¼ C. fresh lime juice

½ C. sour cream

2 T. olive oil

¼ C. water

½ tsp. sea salt

¼ tsp. black pepper

½ tsp. minced garlic (or one garlic clove)

¼ tsp. red pepper flakes

⅛ tsp. cumin

DIRECTIONS

1. Place all ingredients in a blender or food processor; blend until creamy. Store in refrigerator.

NET CARBS 1g - per 2 T. serving				
calories	fat	protein	carbs	fiber
81	8g	1g	3g	2g

condiments

Caesar Dressing

SERVINGS: 28
(1 T. serving size)

You will kick bottled Caesar dressing to the curb after tasting this homemade version. Any time a fresh batch of dressing is made from scratch, it far exceeds the taste over any store-bought brand. You may never use any other Caesar dressing ever again; this one is delicious!

INGREDIENTS

2 anchovy fillets

2 cloves garlic

1 C. mayonnaise

1/3 C. shredded parmesan cheese

¼ C. half & half

1 T. lemon juice

1 T. Dijon mustard

1 tsp. Worcestershire sauce

DIRECTIONS

1. Add anchovy fillets and garlic cloves to a food processor or blender and pulse to a paste.

2. Add remaining ingredients and blend until dressing is creamy. Refrigerate at least 1 hour before serving; keep refrigerated.

janeva's tips

The anchovy fillets are necessary for an authentic Caesar dressing flavor; they add a light and natural saltiness to the dressing -- I freeze any leftover fillets from the tin to use for another time.

NET CARBS 1g - per serving				
calories	fat	protein	carbs	fiber
63	6g	1g	1g	0g

Creamy Alfredo Sauce

SERVINGS: 4

I have been making this Alfredo sauce for several years. To convert it to low carb wasn't necessary, as it is already a perfect low carb sauce – bonus! Try this creamy, cheesy, buttery sauce over Zoodles, pg. 224 in this cookbook or the Cajun Alfredo Shrimp Zoodles, pg. 156.

INGREDIENTS

¼ C. unsalted butter

1 C. heavy whipping cream

½ tsp. minced garlic

⅛ tsp. white pepper

⅛ tsp. salt

¾ C. shredded parmesan cheese

Pinch of nutmeg

DIRECTIONS

1. In a large sauce pan, melt butter over medium heat.

2. Add cream, garlic, salt, pepper and nutmeg; stir.

3. Bring to a low boil and turn heat down to medium low; simmer 4-6 minutes stirring often.

4. Add cheese slowly while stirring (or it will clump); continue to stir for 1-2 minutes until smooth and creamy. Serve hot.

NET CARBS 4g - per serving				
calories	fat	protein	carbs	fiber
387	39g	7g	4g	0g

Easy Homestyle Salsa

SERVINGS: 16
(1/4 C. serving size)

This is a very fresh tasting salsa – a similar salsa to the kind you would find at a Mexican restaurant. It is excellent served over egg dishes, casseroles, Mexican dishes, or any other savory recipe requiring a boost of fresh flavor. For a special treat, I like to eat this as a dip with Quest® tortilla style chips.

INGREDIENTS

1 – 28 oz. can crushed tomatoes

½ medium yellow onion, chopped

1 jalapeno, chopped (seeds and membrane removed)

½ C. fresh cilantro, chopped

1 T. lime juice

1 tsp. minced garlic

½ tsp. cumin

¼ tsp. salt

DIRECTIONS

1. Place all ingredients in a medium mixing bowl; stir to mix. Taste and adjust seasonings, if desired. Keep refrigerated.

janeva's tips

This recipe makes approximately 4 C. salsa and stores for approximately 5 days in the fridge. I freeze 1 C. portions by placing in resealable freezer bags -- remove air from bags before freezing

NET CARBS 2g - per serving				
calories	fat	protein	carbs	fiber
15	0g	0g	3g	1g

Jerk Seasoning

SERVINGS: varies

Excellent Caribbean style seasoning for pork, beef or chicken.

INGREDIENTS

1 T. ground coriander

2 tsp. garlic powder

2 tsp. ground ginger

2 tsp. onion powder

1 tsp. salt

1 tsp. pepper

1 tsp. dried thyme

¾ tsp. ground nutmeg

¾ tsp. ground allspice

½ tsp. ground cinnamon

¼ tsp. cayenne pepper (optional)

DIRECTIONS

1.   Place all ingredients in a medium bowl; stir to mix.
2.   Store in an airtight jar.

janeva's tips

Individual servings sizes are minimal in nutritional count and therefore not included in nutrition info; entire recipe only.

NET CARBS 1g - entire recipe				
calories	fat	protein	carbs	fiber
18	0g	0g	4g	3g

Pico de Gallo

SERVINGS: 5

A perfect condiment for topping casseroles, Mexican dishes, eggs, veggies, or any other dish requiring a boost of flavor.

INGREDIENTS

1½ C. diced fresh Roma tomatoes

1 C. diced red or yellow onion

2/3 C. chopped fresh cilantro

1 - 2 jalapeno peppers, seeded and finely chopped

Juice of ½ lime, or to taste

Sea salt, to taste

DIRECTIONS

1. In a medium bowl, gently combine tomatoes, onion, cilantro and jalapeno pepper.

2. Remove any seeds from the lime half; squeeze juice over the Pico de Gallo mixture. Sprinkle with sea salt; gently mix to blend in juice and salt.

3. Taste the Pico de Gallo Salsa; adjust salt, lime, jalapeno or cilantro as desired. Store in a covered container in refrigerator.

NET CARBS 3g - per ½ cup serving				
calories	fat	protein	carbs	fiber
31	0g	1g	4g	1g

Puttanesca Sauce

SERVINGS: 6

Puttanesca sauce is an Italian tomato-based sauce that became popular in the early 1960's in Naples, Italy, and was typically served over pastas. Spaghetti alla puttanesca translates as 'spaghetti in the style of a prostitute' in Italian (I'm unsure of the reason for that one!) Recipes can often differ according to preferences, but this traditional tomato-based sauce is typically seasoned with capers, anchovies and olives including green, black, or even Kalamata varieties. In this recipe, I simply add green olives, giving it that briny tang. This sauce compliments chicken, fish and seafood, veggie noodles or pizza. For starters, try this one in the Tomato Braised Cauliflower recipe, pg. 220. Delizioso!

INGREDIENTS

28 oz. can peeled whole tomatoes

2 T. tomato paste

¼ tsp. black pepper

2 tsp. onion powder

½ tsp. chili powder

1 tsp. garlic powder

1 T. Italian seasoning

1 tsp. salt

2 T. red wine vinegar

½ tsp. crushed red pepper flakes

2 T. extra virgin olive oil

½ C. sliced green olives (no pimientos)

DIRECTIONS

1. Drain tomatoes and discard juice.

2. Place all ingredients in a blender (except olives); blend until tomatoes are pureed.

3. Pour mixture into a medium saucepan and bring to a low boil over medium high heat. Immediately turn down to medium/low heat; simmer for 25 minutes, stirring occasionally.

4. Add green olives and stir; simmer 5 more minutes. Refrigerate sauce until use.

janeva's tips

This sauce freezes well in an airtight container.

NET CARBS 6g - per serving				
calories	fat	protein	carbs	fiber
93	7g	2g	8g	2g

Rich & Sassy BBQ Sauce

SERVINGS: varies

I cannot find a jarred sauce that tastes better than this homemade version. As the recipe title suggests, it is very rich and sassy, and you won't need much to elevate the flavor of meats. There comes satisfaction as you cook the sauce yourself and smell the smoky-sweet aroma in the kitchen. Delicious served on beef, poultry and pork.

INGREDIENTS

1 C. Heinz® no sugar added ketchup

1 T. olive oil

1 T. onion powder

1 T. lemon juice

1 T. brown sugar alternative (I use Sukrin® Gold or Swerve® brand)

1 tsp. minced garlic

1 tsp. chili powder

1 T. liquid smoke

1 T. apple cider vinegar

½ tsp. salt

¼ tsp. black pepper

DIRECTIONS

1. Add all ingredients to a medium saucepan; stir to mix. Heat on medium/medium high heat until mixture starts to bubble, stirring occasionally.

2. Reduce heat to low and cover. Simmer 15 – 20 minutes, stirring occasionally.

3. Remove cover, and cook to desired thickness, if necessary. Store in fridge.

NET CARBS 0g - based on approx. 1T. serving				
calories	fat	protein	carbs	fiber
16	1g	0g	1g	0g

Spaghizza Sauce

SERVINGS: 6

Spaghetti + Pizza = Spaghizza Sauce. This recipe is perfect for any dish requiring a tomato-based sauce. A good homemade Italian sauce can take several hours to cook, but with this one, it's ready in less than 30 minutes and no one will ever know you didn't spend hours over the stove. It's really that delicious.

INGREDIENTS

28 oz. can crushed tomatoes

2 T. tomato paste

¼ tsp. black pepper

½ tsp. crushed red pepper flakes

1 tsp. onion powder

1 tsp. garlic powder

1 T. dried Italian seasoning

1 tsp. salt

2 T. apple cider vinegar

2 T. extra virgin olive oil

DIRECTIONS

1. Place all ingredients in a blender; blend until tomatoes are pureed.

2. Pour mixture into a medium saucepan, and bring to a low boil.

3. Immediately turn to low heat. Simmer for 25 - 30 minutes, stirring occasionally.

4. Refrigerate sauce until use. Freezes well.

janeva's tips

The longer the sauce is simmered, the thicker it will get. For spaghetti sauce, follow recipe directions above. For pizza sauce simmer 20 – 30 minutes longer to thicken.

NET CARBS 8g - per serving				
calories	fat	protein	carbs	fiber
91	5g	3g	11g	3g

Taco Seasoning

SERVINGS: 8
(recipe makes approximately ½ C. or 8 tablespoons)

Have you checked the ingredients in pre-packaged taco seasoning? Many of them have hidden sugar which is simply a cheap filler and unnecessary for flavor. Try making your own at home with this popular taco seasoning recipe. This homemade version is well balanced and adds excellent flavor to your favorite Mexican dishes.

INGREDIENTS

1 ½ T. chili powder

2 T. cumin

1 ½ T. paprika

1 ½ T. onion powder

1 T. garlic powder

1/8 to ½ tsp. cayenne, or to taste

DIRECTIONS

1. Mix all ingredients together; store in an airtight jar.

janeva's tips

I use one tablespoon taco seasoning to season 1 lb. of meat.

NET CARBS 2g - per serving				
calories	fat	protein	carbs	fiber
11	0g	0g	2g	0g

Teriyaki Sauce

SERVINGS: 20
(approximately 1 T. serving size)

Teriyaki sauce adds an abundance of flavor to a variety of dishes. Try it as a marinade for beef, chicken or pork. It is perfect for adding to stir-fry or any Oriental style recipe. In this recipe, it is important to use the low-sodium soy sauce, or it will be too salty. I recommend tasting the sauce after preparing and adjusting the taste with the ingredients to your liking. This sauce is excellent in the Teriyaki Beef and Broccoli recipe, pg. 150 in this cookbook.

INGREDIENTS

slurry

¼ C. water

¼ tsp. glucomannan powder (konjac powder)

sauce

½ C. + 2 T. low sodium soy sauce or tamari

½ C. water

2 T. cooking sherry

2 tsp. toasted sesame oil

¼ C. maple syrup, sugar free

2 T. brown sugar alternative (Sukrin® Gold or Swerve®)

2 tsp. minced garlic

2 tsp. minced ginger

janeva's tips

I often use minced garlic and ginger from a jar to make preparation quick and easy. These ingredients may be found in the produce section at your local grocers.

DIRECTIONS

1. To make slurry, add water and glucomannan powder to a small bowl. Whisk with a fork until powder is dissolved; set aside.

2. To a medium saucepan, add all sauce ingredients. Bring to a low boil over medium high heat, stirring constantly.

3. Turn heat to medium low. Slowly drizzle slurry mixture into hot teriyaki sauce while stirring.

4. Stir 1-2 minutes while cooking until thickened. Keep refrigerated until ready to use.

NET CARBS 1g - per serving				
calories	fat	protein	carbs	fiber
11	0g	0g	1g	0g

Warm Bacon Dressing

SERVINGS: 8

This dressing is everything the palate could want – it's tangy, salty, sweet and smoky. Perfect for topping a fresh salad such as the Strawberry Fields Salad, pg. 98

INGREDIENTS

3 T. apple cider vinegar or red wine vinegar

¼ C. maple syrup, sugar free

3 T. Dijon mustard

1 tsp. kosher salt

1 tsp. coarse ground black pepper

6 slices bacon, diced into ¼" pieces

1 ½ tsp. minced garlic

DIRECTIONS

1. In a small bowl, whisk together the vinegar, syrup, Dijon mustard, salt and pepper; set aside.

2. Place bacon in a saucepan and cook over medium-low heat 5 minutes. (This will slowly start to render the fat drippings you will be using in the dressing and should not be rushed.)

3. Increase heat to medium and continue cooking bacon, stirring frequently, until bacon is browned and crispy. Remove pan from heat; using a slotted spoon, transfer bacon to paper towels to drain. Keep fat drippings in pan.

4. Return pan to stove top, and add garlic; give it a few stirs. Immediately add dressing mixture, and stir to blend.

5. Bring dressing to a low boil over medium heat. Simmer 1 minute, stirring constantly.

6. Remove from heat, and stir in bacon.

7. Serve immediately, or keep refrigerated until use. Warm dressing in the microwave before serving.

janeva's tips

This dressing is outstanding when served as a sauce over cooked pork.

NET CARBS 3g - per serving (1 T.)				
calories	fat	protein	carbs	fiber
96	8g	3g	3g	0g

flavored compound butters

CINNAMON SUNRISE, LEMON HERB & ZESTY ITALIAN GARLIC

These compound butter recipes landed me as a contestant on the Oprah Winfrey show. For several years I was interested in creating compound butters (flavored butters), both sweet and savory. Since then, I have created and accumulated over 500 original recipes for an extensive variety of compound butters.

In April 2007, the Oprah Winfrey show partnered with QVC television for 'America's Next Big Idea' requesting new ideas from viewers in all categories including gourmet foods. I sent in my compound butter recipe idea and was accepted as a contestant for the show. Off to Los Angeles I went to film the presentation of the flavored butters in front of a QVC judging panel. After the judges tasted the butters, their reply was: "Compound butters would present a challenge when shipping to warm weather regions, but please put them in a store. We would buy them!"

Sweet compound butters are a great addition to have on hand to enhance the flavor of your morning biscuits, toast, pancakes, waffles and muffins. Try the Cinnamon Sunrise Butter (pg. 133) with notes of cinnamon, maple and orange —heavenly. Savory compound butters are perfect for slathering over a whole chicken, melted on top of a grilled steak, and a perfect addition to veggies, egg dishes, soups and more.

janeva's tips

To store, I like to roll the butter in a log making it easy to slice with a sharp knife dipped in hot water. To roll, place a large sheet of plastic wrap on a work surface. Put butter in the center and pull the far end of the plastic wrap up and over to meet the nearest edge where you are standing. Using a straight edge (such as a ruler or edge of a baking sheet), push the butter tightly into a log shape from the bottom edge. Roll up in the plastic wrap and twist ends to seal; this will form it into a cylindrical log shape. Keep refrigerated. Freezes well when wrapped tightly in plastic wrap.

Cinnamon Sunrise Butter

SERVINGS: 16
(1 T. per serving)

Add something special to your baked goods — try this sweet cinnamon butter on low carb breads, scones, muffins, cornbread, pancakes, waffles, or any other baked goods. The addition of maple syrup and orange zest compliment the flavor of this incredibly tasty cinnamon butter.

INGREDIENTS

1 C. (2 sticks) unsalted butter, softened

1 tsp. cinnamon

2 T. sugar free maple syrup

1 T. fresh orange zest or dried orange peel

DIRECTIONS

1. Place all ingredients in a mixing bowl. Stir with a wooden spoon to mix.

2. Store in an airtight container in fridge.

NET CARBS 0g - per serving				
calories	fat	protein	carbs	fiber
104	12g	0g	0g	0g

Lemon Herb Butter

SERVINGS: 16
(1 T. per serving)

A perfect condiment for fish, seafood, poultry, eggs and veggies.

INGREDIENTS

1 C. (2 sticks) unsalted butter, softened

1 ½ T. chopped fresh basil

1 T. chopped fresh chives

2 tsp. chopped fresh tarragon or parsley

1/8 tsp. garlic powder

½ tsp. red pepper flakes

1/8 tsp. sea salt

Zest of 1 lemon

DIRECTIONS

1. To a medium mixing bowl, add all ingredients. Using a stand mixer or electric hand mixer, mix on medium speed until all ingredients are blended. Be careful not to over mix or the butter will aerate and become whipped. (We don't want this.)

2. Store in an airtight container in fridge.

NET CARBS 0g - per serving				
calories	fat	protein	carbs	fiber
103	12g	0g	0g	0g

Zesty Italian Garlic Butter

SERVINGS: 16
(1 T. per serving)

This flavorful compound butter is exceptional on seafood and meats, topping cooked veggies, or spreading on bread and crackers.

INGREDIENTS

1 C. (2 sticks) unsalted butter, softened

¼ C. fresh chopped Italian parsley

1 tsp. garlic powder

2 T. chopped fresh chives

1 tsp. red pepper flakes

½ tsp. sea salt

¼ tsp. black pepper

DIRECTIONS

1. Place all ingredients in a mixing bowl. Stir with a wooden spoon to mix.

2. Store in an airtight container in fridge.

NET CARBS 0g - per serving				
calories	fat	protein	carbs	fiber
103	12g	0g	0g	0g

Main Dishes

contents

Balsamic Beef Roast
crockpot recipe

SERVINGS: 4

We make this recipe at least 2 times per month in our home. It's easy, tasty, and smells darn good cooking in the crockpot all day. Served on the Garlic Mashed Fauxtatoes, pg. 208 in this cookbook, makes it extra special and a full family meal.

INGREDIENTS

3 lb. boneless chuck roast

1 T. kosher salt

1 tsp. black pepper

1 tsp. garlic powder

1 T. olive oil

½ C. balsamic vinegar

2 C. beef broth

½ C. chopped yellow onion

Chopped fresh parsley, to taste (for garnish)

DIRECTIONS

1. Season entire roast with salt, pepper and garlic powder.

2. Heat oil in a large frying pan over medium/medium high heat. Add roast and brown, about 2-3 minutes each side.

3. Place roast in crockpot; add remaining ingredients in and around roast.

4. Cover and cook on low 8 hours or on high for 6 hours.

5. Plate and serve drizzled with juices.

janeva's tips

The balsamic vinegar gives this beef a punch of flavor, but beware the carbs in some brands and be sure to read the nutrition label. I like using Pompeian® brand with only 5 grams carbs per tablespoon.

NET CARBS 10g - per serving				
calories	fat	protein	carbs	fiber
561	27g	73g	11g	1g

French Dip Beef Roast & Fauxtatoes
a family favorite crockpot recipe

SERVINGS: 6

My family has been making this recipe for several years, even before embarking on the low carb lifestyle. It is, by far, our favorite way to make a tender and melt-in-your-mouth beef roast. The radishes add a baby potato-like veggie addition – if you're not fond of radishes (I'm with you there regarding raw radishes), these little red orbs of joy transform themselves during cooking and become mild and tender, losing their red coloring so no one will know they're not potatoes! You may use leftovers (not that there will be any) for sandwiches, burritos, or any other dish requiring flavorful cooked beef.

INGREDIENTS

3 lb. chuck roast or bone-in sirloin roast

¼ C. soy sauce

2 C. beef broth

1 T. Dijon mustard

2 tsp. onion powder

1 tsp. kosher salt

1 tsp. black pepper

1 tsp. minced garlic

2 C. whole red radishes, unpeeled

DIRECTIONS

1. Place all ingredients in the crockpot except roast and radishes; stir to mix.

2. Add roast to crockpot

3. Cut off ends of radishes and discard; add radishes to crockpot. Cover crockpot and cook on low 8-9 hours.

4. Serve drizzled with the au jus (juice) from the beef.

NET CARBS 2g - per serving				
calories	fat	protein	carbs	fiber
541	38g	44g	3g	1g

Glazed Meatloaf

SERVINGS: 8

INGREDIENTS

meatloaf

1 C. shredded zucchini

1 lb. 93% lean ground beef

1 lb. 85% ground beef

2 T. dried minced onions

1 tsp. garlic powder

3 T. Heinz® no sugar added ketchup

2 large eggs, slightly beaten

1/3 C. half and half

1 ½ tsp. sea salt

½ tsp. Italian seasoning

½ tsp. paprika

½ tsp. red pepper flakes

¼ tsp. black pepper

¾ C. pork rind crumbs (see TIP)

sauce

¾ C. Heinz® no sugar added ketchup

2 T. brown sugar substitute (I use Sukrin Gold® or Swerve® brand)

½ tsp. onion powder

¼ tsp. sea salt

¼ tsp. black pepper

The secret ingredient in this juicy meatloaf is the shredded zucchini locking in the moisture. No worries for veggie haters, it won't be detected in flavor and is a perfect way to sneak in some veggies for the kids.

Refrain from allowing the list of ingredients to intimidate, it all mixes up in just one bowl. While the meatloaf bakes, you have plenty of time to whip up a batch of the glaze. I've never been much of a fan of meatloaf until I created this low carb version! Try serving it with the Garlic Mashed Fauxtatoes, pg. 208, for an extra special classic comfort meal.

DIRECTIONS

1. Preheat oven to 375 degrees.

2. Line a 9" x 5" inch loaf pan with parchment paper down the center so parchment hangs over sides. Set aside.

3. Place shredded zucchini on a microwave proof plate and heat on high for 45 seconds. Blot with paper towel, set aside.

4. To a large mixing bowl, add remaining meatloaf ingredients including zucchini; mix just until blended. (Refrain from over mixing or the meatloaf will be dense and tough.)

5. Add meatloaf to pan, and gently press down evenly. Bake 40 minutes.

6. Meanwhile, prepare sauce by adding all ingredients to a bowl; stir to mix. Remove meatloaf from oven and pour sauce evenly over the top.

7. Bake an additional 20 minutes and transfer to a cooling rack. Let rest 10 minutes before slicing.

8. Serve slices drizzled with juice from pan.

janeva's tips

Pork rinds may be ground to crumbs; however, to make it easy, I purchase Pork King Good® brand prepared pork rind crumbs in a jar, found on Amazon.com.

NET CARBS 5g - per serving				
calories	fat	protein	carbs	fiber
298	17g	28g	5g	0g

Mac & Cheeseburger Casserole

SERVINGS: 6

Miss macaroni and cheese? The cauliflower florets in this recipe make a great substitute for the macaroni – it's a deliciously satisfying swap. I could eat this casserole dish every day! Enough said.

INGREDIENTS

6 C. cauliflower florets (about 1 head)

1 ½ lbs. lean ground beef

1 envelope Lipton's® beefy onion soup mix, dry

2 T. unsalted butter

1 C. unsweetened almond milk, plain

½ C. heavy cream

1 tsp. glucomannan powder (konjac powder)

2 ½ C. shredded cheddar jack cheese, divided

Salt and pepper, to taste

DIRECTIONS

1. Preheat oven to 350 degrees.

2. Place cauliflower in a large microwave proof bowl; add 1" inch water. Cover and cook on high 10 - 12 minutes or until fork tender. Drain and return to bowl; set aside.

3. Meanwhile, add ground beef and dry soup mix to a large skillet. Cook until browned. Drain any fat and add beef to cauliflower; set aside.

4. In a medium saucepan, melt butter over low heat. Using a whisk, stir in almond milk and cream and immediately sprinkle in glucomannan powder while stirring.

5. Increase heat to medium. Continue to stir constantly, to thicken, approximately 3 minutes.

6. Remove sauce from heat and stir in 1 ½ C. shredded cheese until blended and smooth. Add cheese sauce to beef and cauliflower mixture; fold to coat and evenly spread mixture in a 9" x 13" inch casserole pan. Season with salt and pepper.

7. Sprinkle casserole with remaining 1 C. cheese.

8. Bake 20 - 25 minutes or until cheese is melted and edges are bubbly. Let rest 5 – 8 minutes before serving.

janeva's tips

Delicious served with Italian Asparagus, pg. 210.

NET CARBS 8g - per serving				
calories	fat	protein	carbs	fiber
503	35g	36g	12g	4g

Pepper Steak

SERVINGS: 2

This recipe is a quick and easy one-pan dish that is beautiful in color and full of flavor. It's a perfect dish for weekdays when you're low on time for making a homemade meal. Sirloin steak is recommended, but I sometimes use ribeye steak for an extra special tender treat.

INGREDIENTS

1 lb. sirloin steak, sliced in ¼" strips

1 ½ C. beef broth, low sodium (divided)

2 T. soy sauce

¼ tsp. allulose granulated sugar substitute

½ tsp. black pepper

1 T. olive oil

½ C. chopped green onion

1 tsp. minced garlic

1 C. sliced assorted bell peppers (green, yellow and red)

½ C. sliced celery

1 C. canned diced tomatoes, drained

DIRECTIONS

1. In a small mixing bowl, mix together 1 C. beef broth, soy sauce, allulose and black pepper. Set aside.

2. Heat oil in a large frying pan over medium/medium high heat.

3. Add steak strips, green onion and garlic; cook till browned but not cooked through.

4. Add broth mixture to pan; simmer uncovered over low heat 20 minutes, stirring occasionally.

5. Add ½ C. beef broth, peppers, celery and tomatoes. Cover and simmer 10 minutes. Serve hot.

janeva's tips

Delicious served over cauliflower rice – easily found in the frozen foods section at your local grocers.

NET CARBS 8g - per serving				
calories	fat	protein	carbs	fiber
411	15g	50g	12g	4g

Reuben Casserole

SERVINGS: 6

My family loves Reuben sandwiches, so I was inspired to create this lasagna-style Reuben recipe with that in mind. This casserole makes great leftovers as well. The way the flavors meld together after it's first bake is delicious.

INGREDIENTS

2 T. salted butter

1 lb. corned beef, chopped (I use shaved deli style)

16 oz. sauerkraut, drained and patted dry

1 C. mayonnaise

1/3 C. ketchup, no sugar added

2 tsp. pickle relish

1 tsp. caraway seeds, divided

8 slices deli Swiss cheese

DIRECTIONS

1. Preheat oven to 350 degrees.

2. In a medium bowl, mix together the mayonnaise, ketchup and relish; set aside.

3. Place butter in an 8" x 8" inch baking pan; microwave on high until melted. Spread evenly over bottom of pan.

4. Evenly place ½ the corned beef in baking dish; spread with ½ the mayonnaise mixture. Top with ½ the sauerkraut; sprinkle with ½ tsp. caraway seeds and 4 slices cheese.

5. Evenly place, in order, the remaining corned beef, sauerkraut, mayonnaise mixture, caraway seeds and cheese slices.

6. Bake 40 minutes.

7. Casserole will have a liquid-y sauce that is delicious; let rest about 5 minutes before cutting. Drizzle sauce over each casserole serving (optional). Serve hot.

NET CARBS 3g - per serving				
calories	fat	protein	carbs	fiber
523	44g	28g	5g	2g

main dishes - beef

Teriyaki Beef & Broccoli

SERVINGS: 4

In the mood for Chinese take-out? Make it at home! This Teriyaki Beef and Broccoli dish is easy to prep and cook. I like serving this with cauliflower rice, which is easily found in the frozen foods section at your local grocer.

INGREDIENTS

1 ½ lbs. sirloin steak, thinly sliced

Salt and pepper, to taste

3 tsp. olive or avocado oil, divided

4 C. broccoli florets

4 T. chopped green onion, divided

½ tsp. red pepper flakes

2 T. water

1/3 C. Teriyaki Sauce, pg. 129

Toasted sesame seeds, to taste (for topping)

DIRECTIONS

1. Heat 1 tsp. oil in a large skillet over medium/medium high heat. Season steak strips with salt and pepper and add to hot skillet. Stir fry steak approximately 3 - 5 minutes or until browned and cooked.   Plate steak and cover to keep warm. Wipe skillet out with a paper towel and return skillet to heat.

2. Add 2 tsp. oil to skillet; heat over medium/medium high heat. Add broccoli florets, 2 T. green onion and red pepper flakes. Cook 3 – 5 minutes or until florets start to brown and soften. Add water to pan; stir fry until water evaporates and veggies are tender crisp.

3. Return beef to skillet. Pour teriyaki sauce over beef and broccoli mixture; heat through.

4. Serve sprinkled with remaining 2 T. green onion and toasted sesame seeds. Serve with additional salt, pepper and teriyaki sauce, if desired.

janeva's tips

Toasted sesame seeds may be found in the seasonings section or ethnic foods aisle at your local grocer.

NET CARBS 3g - per serving				
calories	fat	protein	carbs	fiber
503	27g	46g	5g	2g

main dishes - beef

Zoodle Lasagna
made with spiralized zucchini

SERVINGS: 12

This lasagna is a family recipe we have made for years and it's truly the only lasagna recipe I eat – it's that good. While the original recipe calls for noodles made of pasta, I've simply replaced them with zoodles (zucchini noodles). If you are unfamiliar with how to prepare zoodles, please refer to the Zoodles recipe, pg. 224, for a tutorial on how to spiralize them (you will prepare only, not cook the zoodles before adding to recipe.) This lasagna feeds a small crowd or family, but you may cut the lasagna in serving sizes and freeze for meals at a later time. Your family and friends will rave over this lasagna.

INGREDIENTS

8 C. zoodles (spiralized zucchini noodles), divided

Salt

1 lb. lean ground beef

1 lb. bulk sausage (I use Jimmy Dean®)

1 recipe Spaghizza Sauce, pg. 127

4 C. shredded sharp cheddar cheese, divided

4 C. shredded mozzarella cheese, divided

DIRECTIONS

1. Lay two sets of paper towels on a work surface, about three sheets long and two sheets thick. Spread raw zoodles evenly over towels.

2. Sprinkle zoodles lightly with salt. Roll up zoodles in paper towels and set aside for one hour. This is a necessary step to absorb moisture from the zucchini, or your lasagna will be watery.

3. Preheat oven to 350 degrees.

4. Brown the ground beef and sausage in a large frying pan over medium/medium high heat. Drain and set aside.

5. Spread 4 C. zoodles evenly in the bottom of a 9" x 13" inch casserole pan.

6. Layer ½ the meat mixture over the top of zoodles.

7. Layer ½ the Spaghizza Sauce over the beef.

8. Layer 2 C. of the cheddar and 2 C. of the mozzarella over the sauce.

9. Repeat layers with remaining ingredients.

10. Bake 45 minutes; let rest 10 minutes before cutting and serving.

NET CARBS 10g - per serving				
calories	fat	protein	carbs	fiber
491	19g	37g	12g	2g

Blackened Fish Tacos

SERVINGS: 4

This recipe calls for tilapia fillets, but you may use your favorite white fish in its' place. Here in Minnesota, walleye is the fish of choice for its meaty white texture and clean taste, yet it may not be readily available in your area. Try substituting shrimp for the fish in this recipe as a delicious option as well!

For the tortilla wraps, I use Mission® Carb Balance Soft Taco Flour Tortillas. The tortillas can quickly add carbs to this meal at 17 g net carbs (2 per serving). Just be mindful of other low carb meal choices when adding these tacos to your daily meal and carb count. These tacos are very filling!

INGREDIENTS

slaw

¼ head red cabbage, thinly shredded

2 ½ T. mayonnaise

¼ C. sour cream

1 T. lime juice

½ tsp. garlic powder

½ tsp. hot sauce

fish tacos

1 lb. tilapia fillets

1 T. blackened or Creole seasoning

1 T. olive oil

8 small, low carb soft taco tortilla wraps

toppings (optional)

Sliced or cubed avocado

Chopped Roma tomatoes

Cotija cheese

Chopped fresh cilantro

Red onion, thinly sliced

Lime wedges

DIRECTIONS

1. Make slaw by adding all ingredients to a medium bowl (except cabbage); stir with a whisk to mix. Cover and place in fridge until ready to serve; toss with cabbage just before serving.

2. Wash fish fillets, pat dry and cut into 8 equal pieces. Season both sides with seasoning.

3. In a large frying pan, heat oil over medium/medium high heat. Add fish fillets and fry 2 - 3 minutes each side or until fish flakes easily with a fork. Plate and cover with foil to keep warm.

4. To warm tortillas, heat a dry frying pan or griddle over medium/medium high heat. Place tortillas in pan and heat both sides 30 seconds. Plate and cover with foil to keep warm. This will have to be done in batches.

5. Assemble tacos by evenly filling tortillas with fish, then slaw. Top with desired toppings.

janeva's tips

When dressing the slaw, do so just before serving as you will want the fresh crunch in these tacos. (The dressing will soften the cabbage.) In place of the slaw dressing recipe, you may substitute by using plain red cabbage topped with the Avocado Lime Crema recipe, pg. 118 in this cookbook.

NET CARBS 17g - per serving, 2 tacos (no toppings)				
calories	fat	protein	carbs	fiber
512	19g	41g	44g	27g

Cajun Alfredo Shrimp Zoodles

SERVINGS: 4

Transport yourself to New Orleans with this Cajun inspired dish. If you've ever had the chance to try the foods in Louisiana, they're a real treat and always full of flavor. This recipe requires two additional recipes from the cookbook. No need to feel overwhelmed with that thought; it's actually very quick and easy to prepare following simple directions in the recipe.

INGREDIENTS

2 lbs. medium size raw shrimp, deveined and tails off (thawed)

1 T. Cajun seasoning

1 T. olive oil

1 recipe Creamy Alfredo Sauce, pg. 120

1 recipe Zoodles, pg. 224

¼ C. chopped green onion

DIRECTIONS

1. Make Creamy Alfredo Sauce according to recipe directions. Cover and keep warm in saucepan over very low heat. Stir occasionally while preparing the remainder of the dish.

2. Place cleaned raw shrimp in a medium bowl. Sprinkle Cajun seasoning over shrimp and toss to coat.

3. Heat oil over medium/medium high heat in a large frying pan. Add shrimp and stir fry 4-5 minutes or until shrimp are done. (Refrain from over cooking or shrimp will be tough and rubbery.) Plate and cover with foil to keep warm.

4. Prepare and cook Zoodles according to recipe directions.

5. Toss Zoodles, Alfredo sauce and shrimp in a large bowl and plate. Sprinkle with green onions.

janeva's tips

I like serving this family style in a large serving bowl with a set of salad size serving utensils. Set the bowl in the center of the table and allow family and friends to plate the dish themselves. Cooked or grilled chicken may be substituted for the shrimp.

NET CARBS 9g - per serving				
calories	fat	protein	carbs	fiber
537	44g	26g	11g	2g

Firecracker Shrimp Scramble

SERVINGS: 3-4

One day while gazing into my refrigerator I was inspired by random fresh ingredients and came up with this dish. So glad I did! I've served this for breakfast, brunch and even a quick and light dinner. It is creamy, a little bit spicy and full of flavor — an impressive meal for family and friends.

INGREDIENTS

6 large eggs

1 tsp. lemon juice

1/8 tsp. salt

1/8 tsp. black pepper

8 oz. medium raw shrimp (peeled, deveined and tails off)

Creole or Cajun seasoning, to taste

1 T. salted butter

¼ C. chopped green onion (plus more for garnish)

2 oz. Philadelphia® spicy jalapeno cream cheese

Avocado slices, optional (for garnish)

DIRECTIONS

1. In a medium bowl, whisk together the eggs, lemon juice, salt and pepper; set aside.

2. Pat shrimp dry with a paper towel, and season both sides with Creole or Cajun seasoning.

3. In a large frying pan, melt butter over medium/medium high heat. Add shrimp and stir fry until shrimp is pink, approximately 2 minutes. Add onions and continue to cook 1 minute.

4. Pour egg mixture over shrimp. As eggs begin to set, add cream cheese to the eggs. (I take the tip of a knife and place dollops evenly on top of the eggs.)

5. Continue cooking – pulling, lifting and folding eggs until thickened and no visible liquid egg remains. (Do not stir constantly.)

6. Plate and top with additional chopped green onion and black pepper.

7. Garnish with avocado slices, if desired.

janeva's tips

If the Philadelphia® spicy jalapeno cream cheese cannot be found at the grocers, add 2 tsp. chopped fresh jalapeno to the frying pan when cooking the shrimp and use plain cream cheese when adding to the dish. This dish is very versatile and does not need the shrimp if you're just wanting breakfast eggs -- try different flavors of cream cheese as well!

NET CARBS 2g - per serving, based on 4 servings, no avocado				
calories	fat	protein	carbs	fiber
196	13g	24g	2g	0g

Lemon Herb Butter Salmon

SERVINGS: 2

You may never want to eat salmon any other way again. This salmon dish is so rich and delicious, it's my favorite way to cook and serve it – plus, it's an easy no fail recipe. I balance the richness of the salmon by serving it with steamed green veggies such as asparagus, broccolini or fresh green beans.

INGREDIENTS

2 - 8 oz. salmon fillets

1 tsp. olive oil

Creole seasoning, to taste

2 T. Lemon Herb Butter, pg. 134

DIRECTIONS

1. Rub the salmon fillets with olive oil, and lightly sprinkle with seasoning.

2. Place salmon fillets on a parchment lined baking sheet (skin side down unless salmon is skinless) in a cold oven.

3. Turn oven to 400 degrees; bake 25 minutes. Remove from oven and plate.

4. Place 1 T. lemon herb butter on each fillet to melt just before serving.

janeva's tips

If the lemon herb butter is rolled in a tube shape, use about a ¼" slice for the equivalent of 1 T.

NET CARBS 0g - per serving				
calories	fat	protein	carbs	fiber
530	32g	57g	0g	0g

Parmesan Mayo Salmon

SERVINGS: 2

The mayonnaise in this recipe magically seals in the moisture of the salmon. In years past, cooking salmon intimidated me with the fear that it would be dry and overcooked – if you share those same thoughts, try this fearless recipe – it almost can't be overcooked using these simple directions and ingredients!

INGREDIENTS

2 - 8 oz. salmon fillets, skinless

3 T. mayonnaise

½ tsp. garlic powder

½ tsp. lemon pepper

½ tsp. Creole or Cajun seasoning

1/3 C. shredded fresh parmesan cheese

1 T. chopped green onion (plus more for garnish)

Salt and pepper, to taste

DIRECTIONS

1. Preheat oven to 375 degrees.
2. In a small bowl, mix together the mayonnaise, garlic powder, lemon pepper and Creole seasoning. Add parmesan, stir to mix.
3. Line a baking sheet with parchment paper.
4. Place salmon on baking sheet; evenly spread mayo mixture over both fillets and sprinkle with green onion.
5. Bake 15 minutes.
6. To serve, sprinkle with salt, pepper and additional green onions, if desired.

NET CARBS 3g - per serving				
calories	fat	protein	carbs	fiber
621	38g	62g	3g	0g

Tuscan Butter Fish

SERVINGS: 4

During my travels to Italy, I ate a fish dish that was similar to this recipe and went wild over it. Since then, I've created several fish and tomato-based recipes, but this one I find extra special and wanted to share it with you. This recipe falls into the top three dishes I make for company – not only is it a gorgeous dish, it is incredibly delicious too. I recommend serving this with a crisp lettuce side salad such as Janeva's Simple Salad, pg. 90.

INGREDIENTS

tuscan butter fish

4 – 5 oz. tilapia fillets

Salt and pepper, to taste

2 T. olive or avocado oil

3 T. salted butter

2 tsp. minced garlic

1 ½ C. halved grape or cherry tomatoes

2 C. fresh spinach leaves, stems removed and loosely packed

½ C. heavy whipping cream

¼ C. shredded parmesan cheese

½ tsp. dried basil

toppings (optional)

Fresh chopped parsley, to taste

Toasted pine nuts, to taste*

Lemon wedges

DIRECTIONS

1. Pat fish fillets with a paper towel to dry. Season both sides of fillets with salt and pepper; set aside.

2. In a large skillet, heat oil over medium/medium high heat.

3. When oil is hot, add fish fillets and fry 3 minutes on each side or until fish easily flakes with a fork. Remove fish from skillet and plate; set aside.

4. Add butter to hot skillet; melt. Add minced garlic and tomatoes, and season with salt and pepper. Cook 1 ½ minutes, stirring occasionally.

5. Add fresh spinach to skillet. Gently stir until spinach begins to wilt, about 1 minute.

6. Stir in cream, parmesan cheese and basil and bring mixture to a simmer.

7. Reduce heat to low and simmer 3 minutes, stirring occasionally.

8. Return fish fillets to pan. Continue to cook 2-3 minutes.

9. Plate fish fillets and spoon sauce over fish. Season with salt and pepper. Sprinkle with parsley and pine nuts; squeeze lemon wedge over fish, if desired.

janeva's tips

*To toast pine nuts, heat a small skillet to medium-low heat. Add pine nuts and stir approximately 3 minutes until golden in spots and fragrant. Pine nuts add a delicious and crunchy texture to this dish.

NET CARBS 5g - per serving				
calories	fat	protein	carbs	fiber
473	32g	40g	7g	2g

Fall-off-the-Bone Baby Back Ribs

SERVINGS: 6

This is a super easy, no fail recipe for ribs and the meat will literally fall off the bone, as the title describes. The first time I made these ribs for my picky-eater significant other, he couldn't stop his verbal praises while eating them. When I mentioned I was adding this recipe to the cookbook, he said, "They should go on the first page!" Have no fear making these ribs — your family and friends will think you're a professional chef!

INGREDIENTS

2 racks baby back pork ribs (about 3 ½ lbs. total)

1 T. chili powder

1 tsp. kosher salt

1 tsp. black pepper

1 tsp. garlic powder

1 tsp. onion powder

½ tsp. dry mustard

½ C. Rich & Sassy BBQ Sauce, pg. 126

DIRECTIONS

1. Preheat oven to 250 degrees.

2. Add all seasonings to a bowl. Stir to mix and rub seasoning onto ribs, both sides.

3. Place each rack of ribs onto separate pieces of aluminum foil (shiny side up), large enough to wrap each rack tightly with foil. Place wrapped racks on a large baking sheet.

4. Bake 3 hours.

5. Remove ribs from oven and discard foil. Brush ribs with half of the BBQ sauce. Place oven rack on top rung and broil ribs for 4-5 minutes.

6. Generously brush ribs with remaining BBQ sauce. Serve hot.

janeva's tips

In place of the Rich & Sassy BBQ Sauce, you may use a favorite jarred low carb BBQ sauce.

NET CARBS 1g - per serving				
calories	fat	protein	carbs	fiber
500	36g	36g	2g	1g

Jerk Pork Roast
with apricot butter glaze (crockpot recipe)

SERVINGS: 8

Jerk seasoning has a unique flavor all its' own and when combined with the buttery fruit glaze, it perfectly complements this pork roast. Both savory and sweet flavors balance this melt-in-your-mouth dish.

INGREDIENTS

pork

4 lb. pork butt roast, bone in

1 recipe Jerk Seasoning, pg. 122

1 large onion, sliced or chopped

½ C. beef broth

glaze

½ C. apricot preserves, sugar free (I use Smuckers®)

1 ½ T. apple cider vinegar

1 tsp. minced garlic

2 T. salted butter

DIRECTIONS

pork

1. Rub the entire roast with the Jerk Seasoning mix (using entire recipe); place in crockpot.

2. Add onion and broth around the bottom of roast. Cover and cook on low 8-9 hours.

glaze

1. Add all ingredients to a saucepan. Cook over medium heat until butter is melted, stirring to incorporate; set aside or refrigerate until ready to serve. Heat before serving.

2. To serve, slice pork and drizzle apricot butter glaze over the top.

janeva's tips

Delicious served with the Bacon Roasted Brussels Sprouts, pg. 198. Nutrition info does not include seasoning and is minimal. You will likely have much of the glaze left over, so the nutrition info reflects a higher amount than you may be consuming.

NET CARBS 2g - per serving				
calories	fat	protein	carbs	fiber
585	44g	40g	7g	5g

Kalua Pork & Cabbage
crockpot recipe

SERVINGS: 4

Kalua is a traditional Hawaiian cooking method that utilizes a unique underground oven to cook Kalua pig which is often served at luaus. This crockpot recipe has a similar flavor to the traditional tender and smoky flavored pork that is often pulled apart after cooking. I'd recommend suggestions for leftovers, but there won't be any!

INGREDIENTS

pork

3 lb. boneless pork shoulder roast

1 T. kosher salt

1 tsp. black pepper

1 tsp. garlic powder

2 tsp. dried minced onion

1 tsp. dried ginger powder

sauce

1 T. soy sauce

2 tsp. Worcestershire sauce

1 tsp. liquid smoke flavoring

veggies

3 C. shredded green cabbage

3 C. shredded red cabbage

DIRECTIONS

1. Mix together all dry spices and rub over entire pork roast. Place roast in crockpot.

2. In a small bowl, stir together sauce ingredients. Pour over pork roast.

3. Cook covered on high 7-8 hours or cook on low 9-10 hours.

4. Two hours before end of cook time, remove roast; add cabbage and stir to coat with juices. Return roast to crockpot and continue cooking according to above cook times.

NET CARBS 8g - per serving				
calories	fat	protein	carbs	fiber
558	27g	68g	11g	3g

Orange Rosemary Pork Tenderloins

SERVINGS: 4

Basting these tenderloins with fresh orange-rosemary butter truly elevates this pork to another level – it's perfectly tender and melts-in-your-mouth. I make this recipe often and find it's an excellent dish for serving guests – simple to make, yet elegant in flavor. I recommend serving this dish with the Loaded Baked Cauliflower Mash, pg. 212, or simply a steamed green veggie such as broccolini or green beans.

INGREDIENTS

2 – 1 lb. boneless pork tenderloins

Salt and pepper, to taste

½ C. (1 stick) salted butter, softened

1 T. fresh orange zest or dried orange peel

1 tsp. minced garlic

1 T. chopped fresh rosemary leaves

1 C. chicken broth

janeva's tips

I highly recommend using fresh orange zest over dried orange peel for the best flavor in this recipe.

DIRECTIONS

1. Preheat oven to 350 degrees.

2. Place a metal cooling rack on top of a 9" x 13" inch casserole pan to create a raised baking rack for the pork tenderloins; set aside.

3. Season pork tenderloins with salt and pepper on all sides; set aside.

4. To a medium bowl, add butter, orange zest, garlic and rosemary; mix until blended.

5. Add 2 T. of the butter mixture to a large skillet and melt over medium/medium high heat. Add pork tenderloins to skillet and brown all sides. (This takes about 8-10 minutes.)

6. Remove skillet from heat and transfer tenderloins onto the cooling rack/pan assembly.

7. Add chicken broth to skillet and stir to get crusty bits from skillet, then pour into the casserole pan.
    (This creates a steam bath to tenderize the pork while it cooks.)

8. Baste each tenderloin with 1 tsp. butter mixture and place tenderloins into oven on center rack.

9. Roast 20 minutes. Remove and baste each tenderloin with 1 tsp. butter mixture. Roast an additional 15 – 20 minutes. Remove cooked tenderloins and baste each tenderloin with 1 tsp. butter mixture. Let rest.

10. Add 3 T. juice drippings to the remaining butter and stir to melt. Slice tenderloin, and serve drizzled with butter mixture.

NET CARBS 1g - per serving				
calories	fat	protein	carbs	fiber
479	31g	48g	1g	0g

Pork Chops Paprikash

SERVINGS: 2

If you're looking for something different to make with pork chops, this rustic dish is highly recommended! The recipe may easily be doubled or tripled for a great family meal.

INGREDIENTS

2 pork chops, bone-in center cut (approximately 6 oz. each and ½" thick)

½ tsp. garlic powder

½ tsp. salt

½ tsp. black pepper

1 ¼ tsp. paprika, divided

2 T. butter

2 C. thinly sliced yellow onion

½ C. sauerkraut, drained and patted dry

3 T. sour cream

DIRECTIONS

1. Preheat broiler; place oven rack on the 2nd rung position or 4-5" from heat source.

2. Season both sides of the pork chops with garlic powder, salt, pepper, and 1 tsp. paprika (reserving 1/4 tsp. for later.) Place seasoned pork chops on a broiling pan and set aside.

3. In a large frying pan over medium/medium high heat, melt butter. Add onions and cook, stirring frequently, about 8-10 minutes or until lightly browned and caramelized. (After caramelizing, turn burner down to low, keeping warm until ready to serve.)

4. Meanwhile, broil pork chops 4-5 minutes each side. Cover and set aside to rest 5 minutes.

5. Add sauerkraut to onions; heat through. Add sour cream and remaining ¼ tsp. paprika; stir to mix.

6. Plate the onion mixture and serve the pork chops on top.

NET CARBS 5g - per serving				
calories	fat	protein	carbs	fiber
403	14g	37g	8g	3g

Bruschetta Chicken

SERVINGS: 2

This is one of my top favorite chicken recipes, and I have been making this for years, even previously to the low carb lifestyle. Luck has it that it is low carb, so I keep this in my rotation of meals during the month. A dear friend of mine supplies me with tomatoes and fresh basil from her garden from time to time, making this dish garden fresh and extra special.

INGREDIENTS

2 large chicken breasts, boneless & skinless

¾ tsp. sea salt

½ tsp. black pepper

2 T. avocado or olive oil, divided

1 ½ tsp. minced garlic

2 C. baby heirloom tomatoes or cherry tomatoes

1/3 C. balsamic vinegar

¼ C. packed and finely chopped fresh basil

DIRECTIONS

1. Place chicken breasts in a large resealable plastic bag. Using a meat mallet, pound chicken evenly to ½" thick. Season with salt and pepper; set aside.

2. In a large frying pan, heat 1 T. oil over medium/medium high heat. Cook chicken 3 minutes on both sides. Plate and cover to keep warm.

3. Add the remaining 1 T. oil to the same pan. Add the garlic and cook 30 seconds, stirring constantly.

4. Add tomatoes and balsamic vinegar. Cover and cook, stirring occasionally, until tomatoes start to burst and vinegar has thickened, about 7 – 10 minutes.

5. Plate the chicken, top with tomatoes and balsamic vinegar mixture, and sprinkle with fresh basil.

janeva's tips

A reminder to read the balsamic vinegar nutrition label as they can vary greatly with carbs. I like to use Pompeiian® brand that is lower in carbs per tablespoon; delicious too!

NET CARBS 13g - per serving				
calories	fat	protein	carbs	fiber
324	18g	27g	15g	2g

Butter Chicken

SERVINGS: 4

Butter chicken originated in Delhi, India, sometime during the 1950s. The dish was developed by three Indian restaurateurs, and the dish was made "by chance" by mixing the leftover chicken in a tomato gravy, rich in butter and cream; there are many variations of Butter Chicken today based on individual preference. In this recipe, the richness of the tomato gravy comes from heavy whipping cream, coconut milk or Greek yogurt. Delicious served over cauliflower rice (see tip comments), or try it over the Garlic Mashed Fauxtatoes, pg. 208 in this cookbook.

INGREDIENTS

2 T. coconut or olive oil

1 medium onion, chopped

1 ½ tsp. minced garlic

1 tsp. minced fresh ginger

3 large chicken breasts (boneless & skinless), cut in 1" chunks

1 6 oz. can tomato paste

1 T. garam masala

1 tsp. mustard seeds

1 tsp. cumin

1 tsp. chili powder

1 tsp. salt

¼ tsp. black pepper

1 C. heavy whipping cream, coconut milk, or low carb Greek yogurt

Fresh chopped cilantro, to taste (for garnish)

Chopped green onion, to taste (for garnish)

DIRECTIONS

1. In a large frying pan, heat oil over medium/medium high heat. When oil is hot, add chopped onions and cook until light golden brown.

2. Add garlic and ginger. Cook 30 seconds, stirring constantly. Refrain from cooking longer as garlic can burn and get bitter quickly.

3. Immediately add chicken, tomato paste, and spices. Continue to stir fry 6 minutes.

4. Add the cream, milk or yogurt and stir into chicken mixture. Turn down heat to medium low; simmer an additional 8 minutes, stirring often.

5. Plate and garnish with cilantro and green onions, if desired.

janeva's tips

If serving the Butter Chicken over cauliflower rice, I like using the frozen pre-made cauliflower rice from the local grocer. It's quick and easy and there are now several brands readily available for purchase.

NET CARBS 10g - per serving, no garnishes				
calories	fat	protein	carbs	fiber
324	12g	42g	13g	3g

Carolina BBQ Chicken

SERVINGS: 2

What makes this BBQ chicken a Carolina version is the Dijon mustard, adding a flavorful twist to the sauce. Bone in, skin on thighs were chosen for this recipe to amp up the flavor and tenderness of the chicken.

INGREDIENTS

4 chicken thighs, bone in and skin on

Salt and pepper, to taste

¼ C. Rich & Sassy BBQ sauce, pg. 126

¼ C. Dijon mustard

¼ C. maple syrup, sugar free

1 tsp. garlic powder

2 T. apple cider vinegar

DIRECTIONS

1. Preheat oven to 400 degrees.

2. Salt and pepper both sides of the chicken thighs and place in a pie pan or 8" x 8" inch square baking dish; set aside.

3. Place the BBQ sauce, mustard, maple syrup and garlic powder in a bowl. Stir to mix.

4. Pour sauce mixture over chicken thighs, covering completely. Drizzle with vinegar.

5. Bake uncovered 40 minutes.

janeva's tips

You may choose a bottled low carb BBQ sauce in place of making your own as suggested in the recipe; however, there is nothing better than a fresh batch of smoky homemade BBQ sauce. I always have a fresh batch in my fridge for making quick and easy meals like this one.

NET CARBS 7g - per serving				
calories	fat	protein	carbs	fiber
436	28g	34g	7g	0g

Cashew & Bok Choy Chicken

SERVINGS: 2

You may never yearn for take-out Chinese ever again after making this recipe. It's fresh, delicious, and you won't have to worry about any added or hidden ingredients that can jack up the carb count. Delicious served over cauliflower rice — most grocers now carry a steam bag of cauliflower rice in the frozen foods section to make it extra easy!

INGREDIENTS

½ C. whole cashews

1 lb. chicken thighs (boneless and skinless), thinly sliced

Salt and pepper, to taste

1 T. olive oil

5 C. baby bok choy, thinly sliced

1 ½ tsp. minced garlic

¼ tsp. red pepper flakes

2 T. soy sauce

¼ C. chopped fresh cilantro

Hot sauce, to taste (optional)

DIRECTIONS

1. Roast cashews in a large frying pan over medium/medium high heat by stirring constantly about 1-2 minutes, or until light golden brown. Remove from pan and break into halves; set aside.

2. Heat oil in the frying pan over medium high heat.

3. Add the chicken in a single layer and season with salt and pepper; cook for 3 minutes. Flip chicken and place the remaining ingredients on top (except cashews and hot sauce) and cook for an additional 3 minutes without stirring.

4. Cook an additional 3 minutes while stir frying.

5. Serve topped with cashews. Sprinkle with hot sauce, if desired.

NET CARBS 11g - per serving				
calories	fat	protein	carbs	fiber
575	35g	54g	14g	3g

Cowboy Chicken

SERVINGS: 2

This chicken requires some marinating time so keep that in mind for prepping and before cooking. I like to prepare this dish the morning we plan to eat it for dinner that same day, or prep the evening before and let marinate in the fridge overnight. The chipotle peppers, green chiles and Monterrey Jack cheese are full of Southwestern flavor and just the kind that cowboys like.

INGREDIENTS

2 large chicken breasts, boneless & skinless

2 T. olive oil, divided

2 whole chipotle peppers in sauce (canned)

3 T. lime juice

1 tsp. minced garlic

1 tsp. ground cumin

1 tsp. salt

½ tsp. black pepper

1 - 7 oz. can whole roasted and peeled mild green chiles, drained

1 C. shredded Monterey jack cheese

DIRECTIONS

1. Place chicken in a large resealable bag. Using a meat mallet, pound chicken breasts ½" inch thick. Set aside.

2. In a small bowl, place 1 T. olive oil, chipotle peppers, lime juice, garlic, cumin, salt and pepper; stir to mix.

3. Pour marinade mixture into bag with chicken and remove as much air as possible. Seal and marinate in fridge 4 hours or overnight.

4. Heat remaining 1 T. oil in a large skillet or grill pan. When oil is hot, remove chicken from marinade (discard marinade). Cook chicken 3-4 minutes each side.

5. Meanwhile, slice the green chiles open and lay flat on grill or fry pan; char both sides.

6. Top chicken evenly with green chiles. Sprinkle with cheese. To melt the cheese, you may cover until melted, or place under the broiler to brown.

janeva's tips

You will have leftover chipotle peppers from the can. I separate them into 2 pepper portions and freeze for later use.

NET CARBS 10g - per serving				
calories	fat	protein	carbs	fiber
598	34g	56g	15g	5g

French Onion Chicken

SERVINGS: 2

This recipe has become a favorite in our family and is also a very impressive meal to serve to guests as well. It may easily be doubled or tripled to accommodate larger gatherings. I like to serve this dish with fresh steamed green beans and toasted crusty low carb buns slathered in butter — I highly recommend the Rustic Rolls on pg. 40!

INGREDIENTS

2 chicken breasts, boneless and skinless

1 ½ T. butter, divided

1 ½ T. olive oil, divided

2 medium-large yellow onions, sliced

¼ tsp. dried thyme

1/3 C. beef broth

3 T. shredded mozzarella cheese

3 T. shredded gruyere cheese

3 T. shredded parmesan cheese

Salt and pepper, to taste

DIRECTIONS

1. Place chicken breasts in a large plastic resealable bag (or between two sheets of plastic wrap). Using a meat mallet, pound breasts to ½" thick. Season with salt and pepper on both sides and set aside.

2. In a medium frying pan, melt 1 T. butter and 1 T. olive oil over medium heat. When butter is melted, add onions and sprinkle with thyme. Lightly season with salt and pepper.

3. Stir fry onions until deep golden brown and caramelized; this will take about 12-15 minutes. Add beef broth and turn burner to low; cover to keep warm.

4. Meanwhile, add remaining oil and butter to a separate large frying pan over medium/medium high heat. Add chicken breasts; cook 3-4 minutes each side, and turn off burner.

5. Top each chicken breast with ¼ of the onion mixture.

6. Sprinkle cheeses on top of breasts, and cover pan until cheese melts.

7. Evenly plate remaining onion mixture on plates and top with chicken breasts. Season with salt and pepper, if necessary.

NET CARBS 9g - per serving				
calories	fat	protein	carbs	fiber
552	30g	56g	11g	2g

main dishes - poultry

Grilled Hawaiian Chicken

This chicken is a staple go-to recipe when friends come for a visit and is always loved by all. The recipe may be doubled or tripled (or more) very easily if making for a group. What I like most, other than the extraordinary taste, is that I'm not fussing in the kitchen while company is present. While we typically grill this outdoors, it may also be made on a stove top grill pan. Check out those alternative directions below the recipe.

Super simple ingredients and easy to prepare - just give yourself a few hours for marinating the chicken beforehand. There are pineapple rings in this recipe which are typically high in carbs; however, only one ring is used per serving for a total of 9 grams carbs per serving of Hawaiian Chicken. No need to give up pineapple!

SERVINGS: 2

INGREDIENTS

2 large chicken breasts, boneless and skinless

1/3 C. teriyaki sauce, pg. 129

2 pineapple rings (canned in natural juices)

2 slices deli provolone cheese

janeva's tips

This recipe may easily be doubled or tripled for larger gatherings.

DIRECTIONS

1. Place chicken breasts in a large resealable plastic bag. Using a meat mallet, pound chicken evenly to ½" thick. Add teriyaki sauce and marinate in fridge 4 hours or overnight.

2. Heat coals to medium. Grill chicken directly over coals approximately 4-5 minutes each side.

3. Meanwhile, grill pineapple rings over direct heat to char each side, approximately 1-2 minutes each side. Set aside.

4. Move cooked chicken off direct heat and to outer edge of grill. Place one slice of provolone cheese on each breast; top with pineapple ring. Close grill lid to melt cheese.

Alternative Stove Top Method:

1. Follow direction #1 above.

2. Heat 1 T. olive oil in a frying pan or stove top grill pan over medium/medium high heat. Add chicken and cook 3 minutes each side. (You will need to add the oil to the nutritional value for this method.)

3. Follow direction #3 the same as above, on stove top grill.

4. Place one slice of provolone cheese on each chicken breast; top with pineapple ring. Cover or let rest until cheese is melted.

NET CARBS 9g - per serving				
calories	fat	protein	carbs	fiber
397	14g	56g	10g	1g

Mom's Chicken Broccoli Bake

SERVINGS: 8

This is a family favorite my mom often made for our family when I was growing up, and I've continued to enjoy it through the years. The original version was a bit too high in carbs, but it was important to me to keep this traditional dish in my low carb lifestyle. I've made a few revisions to the dish and no one has been the wiser — it's just as delicious and comforting as the original recipe. I hope your family enjoys it as much as mine does!

INGREDIENTS

24 oz. frozen chopped broccoli

1 – 3 lb. whole chicken, cooked (I use a deli rotisserie chicken)

2 C. finely shredded sharp cheddar cheese

1 – 10.5 oz. can Campbell's® condensed cream of chicken soup

½ C. mayonnaise

1 C. diced jicama

1 can (2.8 oz.) crispy fried onions (I use French's®)

Cooking spray

DIRECTIONS

1. Preheat oven to 350 degrees.

2. Remove meat from chicken and cut into bite size pieces. Set aside.

3. Place broccoli in a microwave proof bowl; cook on high 5 minutes. Drain.

4. Evenly spread broccoli in a sprayed 9" x 13" inch casserole pan. Layer with chopped chicken followed by the shredded cheese.

5. In a bowl, mix together the chicken soup and mayonnaise. Evenly spread over cheese.

6. Sprinkle the diced jicama over mayonnaise mixture.

7. Cover and bake 40 minutes. Remove from oven and sprinkle with fried onions. Bake uncovered an additional 10 minutes.

NET CARBS 12g - per serving				
calories	fat	protein	carbs	fiber
510	37g	30g	15g	3g

main dishes - poultry

Turkey Taco Cabbage Skillet

SERVINGS: 2

If you're looking for a quick and easy recipe, this one-pan skillet dish is delicious, filling, and full of flavor. Adding the Mexican inspired toppings makes it even better.

INGREDIENTS

Turkey Taco Cabbage Skillet

1 lb. ground turkey (or beef or chicken)

2 T. Taco Seasoning, pg. 128

1 T. avocado oil

2 C. thinly sliced green cabbage

2 C. thinly sliced red cabbage

½ C. chopped green onion

toppings (optional)

Pico de Gallo, pg. 123

Easy Homestyle Salsa, pg. 121

Shredded cheddar cheese

Sour cream or Mexican crema

Chopped fresh cilantro

Hot sauce

DIRECTIONS

1. To a large skillet over medium/medium high heat, add ground beef and taco seasoning; brown. Drain fat, remove ground beef from pan and set aside.

2. To same frying pan, add oil. When hot, add cabbage and green onion. Stir fry until cabbage is softened and wilted, approximately 10-12 minutes.

3. Add ground beef, heat through.

4. Serve with toppings, if desired.

janeva's tips

Toppings not included in nutritional info. This dish is delicious with or without the toppings. Nutrition info will change if subbing chicken or beef for the turkey in this recipe.

NET CARBS 11g - per serving				
calories	fat	protein	carbs	fiber
396	11g	56g	17g	6g

Veggies

contents

Bacon & Mushroom Celery Root Hash

SERVINGS: 2

If you're fond of a traditional potato hash, give this lower carb version a try. It's every bit as tasty, and the celery root takes on a potato-like flavor and texture.

INGREDIENTS

2 C. cubed celery root (1/2" cubes)

5 slices bacon

1 T. butter

1 ½ C. sliced baby bella mushrooms

½ C. chopped green onion

1 tsp. garlic powder

½ tsp. onion powder

Salt & pepper, to taste

DIRECTIONS

1. Place cubed celery root in a large microwave proof bowl, and cover with water. Microwave on high 5 minutes; drain and set aside.

2. Meanwhile, cut bacon into ½" inch pieces. Fry in a large frying pan over medium heat, stirring and cooking until crisp.

3. Take fry pan off heat and remove cooked bacon with a slotted spoon (reserve bacon grease in pan); drain bacon bits on paper towels and set aside.

4. Place frying pan with bacon grease back on burner and add butter, celery root, garlic powder and onion powder. Cover and fry over medium/medium high heat, stirring occasionally, until celery root is browned and fork tender.

5. Add mushrooms and green onion. Stir fry until mushrooms are browned and cooked; add cooked bacon and heat through. Season with salt and pepper before serving.

janeva's tips

Celery Root Hash is a hashbrown style side dish low in carbs in comparison to standard potatoes. Delicious served with steak and eggs

NET CARBS 15g - per serving				
calories	fat	protein	carbs	fiber
285	15g	15g	22g	7g

Bacon Roasted Brussels Sprouts

SERVINGS: 4

This recipe is dedicated to those who are convinced they don't like Brussels sprouts. The key to making them exceptionally delicious is cooking the heck out of them until they're deep brown in color. It will bring out the nutty caramelized flavor that is so pleasing to the palate — plus, bacon makes everything better, right?

INGREDIENTS

1 lb. thick cut bacon

2 lbs. Brussels sprouts

DIRECTIONS

1. Preheat oven to 400 degrees.

2. Line a large baking sheet with aluminum foil. In one layer, lay bacon strips on sheet (you may have to do this in batches).

3. Bake 12 – 15 minutes or until deep golden brown; you do not have to flip the bacon during baking. Transfer bacon to a plate lined with paper towels to drain grease (you will be using the same pan with bacon grease for the sprouts, so don't discard.) Chop bacon into bite-size pieces. Set aside.

4. Meanwhile, cut root end off Brussels sprouts, and cut in half. Lay sprouts, cut side down, in bacon grease in same pan as bacon was cooked.

5. Roast sprouts 20 minutes; remove from oven and turn sprouts over. Roast an additional 10-15 minutes or until deep golden brown.

6. Place in a serving bowl; sprinkle with chopped bacon.

NET CARBS 9g - per serving				
calories	fat	protein	carbs	fiber
258	14g	21g	18g	9g

veggies

Broccoli Almondine
with lemon butter

SERVINGS: 3-4

This veggie recipe makes a perfect side dish for any main meal and goes with just about any protein whether beef, pork, poultry or fish and seafood. The richness of the butter and crunch of the almonds makes steamed broccoli crave-able!

INGREDIENTS

6 C. broccoli florets (cut in bite size pieces)

¼ C. salted butter

2 T. chopped green onion

2 tsp. lemon juice

Pinch of sea salt

¼ tsp. black pepper

¼ C. sliced or chopped almonds

DIRECTIONS

1. Place broccoli in a large microwave proof bowl; add ¼" inch water.

2. Cover and cook on high 4 minutes or until fork tender. Drain, if necessary.

3. Meanwhile, melt butter in a small saucepan over medium heat. When butter is melted, add onions, lemon juice, salt and pepper; cook approximately 2 minutes, stirring constantly.

4. Remove from heat and stir in almonds.

5. Drizzle lemon butter mixture over broccoli, and gently fold to coat.

NET CARBS 4g - per serving based on 4 servings				
calories	fat	protein	carbs	fiber
182	14g	3g	8g	4g

Cheesy Oven 'Potatoes'

SERVINGS: 4

Cheese, butter, sour cream and 'potatoes' – what's not to like? The cauliflower in this dish takes on a potato-like flavor – even veggie haters will swoon over this dish.

INGREDIENTS

3 C. coarsely riced cauliflower*

2 C. shredded extra sharp white cheddar cheese, divided

¼ C. half & half

2 T. sour cream

2 T. butter

½ tsp. onion powder

Salt and pepper, to taste

DIRECTIONS

1. Preheat oven to 350 degrees.

2. Place riced cauliflower in a microwave safe bowl. Add enough water to cover cauliflower; cover bowl and microwave 8 - 10 minutes or until fork tender. Drain.

3. Place rice in a tea towel and squeeze over sink to remove water from cauliflower; set aside.

4. Meanwhile, to a medium saucepan, add half & half, sour cream, butter and onion powder. Cook over medium/medium low heat, stirring constantly, until melted and creamy.

5. Add 1 ½ C. shredded cheese to saucepan reserving ½ cup (for topping 'potatoes'). Continue to stir until cheese is melted and mixture is creamy.

6. Fold cauliflower into cheese mixture until coated; add to an 8"x 8" inch square or round casserole dish.

7. Sprinkle remaining ½ C. shredded cheese over cauliflower mixture and season with salt and pepper; bake 20 - 25 minutes or until lightly browned.

janeva's tips

*To rice cauliflower, add florets to a food processor and pulse to coarse rice-size bits. As an alternative, you may use a grater and grate by hand.

NET CARBS 4g - per serving				
calories	fat	protein	carbs	fiber
325	27g	16g	6g	2g

Creamed Spinach

SERVINGS: 4

You may never look at spinach the same way again. This creamed spinach is so rich and delicious; it pairs perfectly with a simple grilled burger, steak, pork chop or chicken breast. We often just top our protein with this instead of serving on the side. While I'm not the biggest spinach fan, I find this dish incredible.

INGREDIENTS

¼ C. unsalted butter

½ medium yellow onion, chopped

2 tsp. minced garlic

3 oz. cream cheese

½ C. heavy whipping cream

2 pinches nutmeg

2 pinches cayenne pepper

10 oz. fresh baby spinach

Salt and pepper, to taste

DIRECTIONS

1. In a large skillet, melt butter over medium heat.
2. Add onion; cook until translucent and lightly caramelized, stirring often. Stir in garlic, and cook for 30 seconds.
3. Add cream cheese, heavy cream, nutmeg and cayenne pepper. Stir until cream cheese is melted.
4. Add spinach; stir and cook until spinach is wilted. Taste, and season with salt and pepper, if necessary.
5. Serve as a side or over your favorite grilled meat(s).

NET CARBS 4g - per serving				
calories	fat	protein	carbs	fiber
303	30g	4g	6g	2g

veggies

French Onion Zoodle Gratin

SERVINGS: 2-3

I could eat this veggie side dish as a meal – it's that good. But if I must, I serve it with a grilled steak, chicken breast or pork chop – something that complements it but doesn't compete with it. There's truly one word to describe this cheesy, caramelized onion zoodle dish – droolworthy!

INGREDIENTS

2 ½ C. zoodles (spiralized zucchini noodles)*

2 T. unsalted butter

1 C. thinly sliced yellow onion

½ tsp. chopped fresh thyme (+ more for garnish)

1 tsp. allulose granular sugar substitute

¼ C. beef broth

2 tsp. Worcestershire sauce

Salt and pepper, to taste

1 C. shredded fontina cheese

Cooking spray

DIRECTIONS

1. Roll up zoodles in several paper towels to absorb moisture; set aside.

2. In a medium frying pan, melt butter over medium heat. Add onions and cook for 3-4 minutes or just until starting to lightly brown, stirring constantly.

3. Add thyme, allulose, beef broth and Worcestershire sauce. Sprinkle with salt and pepper. Cook an additional 3-4 minutes until onions are caramelized.

4. Place zoodles and onion mixture in a bowl; toss to evenly mix.

5. Spray a standard size bread loaf pan (approximately 8 ¼" x 4 ¼"). Add zoodle mixture.

6. Sprinkle with fontina cheese and bake 23-25 minutes or until cheese is lightly browned and melted.

7. Let rest a few minutes before serving. Taste and season with additional salt and pepper, if necessary.

janeva's tips

* To make zoodles, see more information for Zoodles, pg. 224. I like to purchase the zoodles pre-made in the veggie section at the grocers. This gives them time to sweat the moisture out so this dish isn't watery – at all! If it does get watery with freshly spiralized zucchini, just pour out any liquid before cutting and serving.

NET CARBS 5g - per serving based on 3 servings				
calories	fat	protein	carbs	fiber
260	22g	13g	5g	2g

Garlic Mashed Fauxtatoes

SERVINGS: 4

These mashed cauliflower fauxtatoes are rich, creamy and flavorful — you won't even know they're not real potatoes! In fact, I served them to a veggie hater and he loved them so much they gave him goosebumps!

INGREDIENTS

fauxtatoes

8 C. cauliflower florets (about 1 large head cauliflower)

2 T. unsalted butter, softened

1 oz. cream cheese, softened

¼ C. grated parmesan cheese

½ tsp. garlic powder

½ tsp. salt

1/8 tsp. black pepper

toppings (optional)

Unsalted butter, to taste

Chopped fresh chives, to taste

Salt and pepper, to taste

DIRECTIONS

1. Place cauliflower in a microwave proof bowl; add 2" inches of water. Cover and cook on high 10-12 minutes or until fork tender; drain. Depending on size of microwave and bowl, you may have to do this in batches.

2. Line a baking sheet with several paper towels, add drained cauliflower. Press down with several more paper towels to absorb moisture.

3. Add cauliflower and all remaining ingredients for fauxtatoes to a food processor and pulse until blended.

4. Serve fauxtatoes topped with pats of butter, chopped chives and additional salt and pepper, if desired.

NET CARBS 6g - per serving, no toppings				
calories	fat	protein	carbs	fiber
140	10g	5g	9g	3g

veggies

Italian Asparagus

SERVINGS: 4

It's amazing how simple ingredients can taste so good. If you're looking for a quick and tasty veggie side dish, this is the one. While I recommend serving this recipe hot from the skillet, I even like to eat it cold as leftovers.

INGREDIENTS

3 T. unsalted butter

4 C. (about 1 bunch) asparagus cut in 1-2" pieces

1 tsp. dried Italian seasoning

1 tsp. minced garlic

½ tsp. kosher salt

¼ tsp. black pepper

2 T. chopped green onion, divided

DIRECTIONS

1. In a large skillet, melt butter over medium/medium high heat.

2. Add asparagus and gently stir fry 5 – 7 minutes or until fork tender.

3. Add remaining ingredients using only 1 T. of the green onion. Reduce heat to medium and stir fry an additional 2 minutes.

4. Sprinkle with remaining 1 T. green onion before serving.

NET CARBS 3g - per serving				
calories	fat	protein	carbs	fiber
105	9g	3g	6g	3g

Loaded Baked Cauliflower Mash

SERVINGS: 6

This recipe is inspired by my love of loaded potato skins. While they are not low carb friendly, this casserole-style version takes on their flavor — and I eat them free of guilt! For a hearty and comfort-food meal, I like serving this dish with the Carolina BBQ Chicken recipe, pg. 180.

INGREDIENTS

8 C. cauliflower florets (bite size)

1 ¼ C. shredded sharp cheddar cheese, divided

¼ C. sour cream

½ tsp. onion powder

¼ C. salted butter

Salt and pepper, to taste

6 slices bacon, cooked and crumbled

1 green onion, chopped

Cooking spray

DIRECTIONS

1. Preheat oven to 400 degrees.

2. Place cauliflower in a large microwave proof bowl. Add 1" inch water; cover and microwave on high 10-12 minutes or until fork tender. Drain. (You may have to do this process in a few batches).

3. Place cauliflower in the center of a kitchen towel. Pull all four corners up to hold and twist in a ball. Squeeze out excess water until cauliflower is almost dry.

4. To a large mixing bowl add cauliflower, 1 C. cheddar cheese, sour cream and onion powder. Stir to mix.

5. Evenly spread cauliflower mixture in a sprayed 8" x 8" inch baking dish; season with salt and pepper. Dot with butter and evenly sprinkle with bacon, green onion and the remaining ½ C. cheddar cheese.

6. Bake 20 minutes.

janeva's tips

Cauliflower may be cooked in advance up to 2 days prior to assembly and stored in fridge until ready to use in the recipe. Frozen cauliflower may also be used and cooked according to package directions; drain and squeeze out water as directed above.

NET CARBS 7g - per serving				
calories	fat	protein	carbs	fiber
275	22g	13g	10g	3g

veggies

Oriental
Green Beans

SERVINGS: 4

This recipe is similar to a dish my mom would often make for the family. While green peas were what the original recipe required, I subbed green beans as a lower carb option, and they are every bit as delicious!

INGREDIENTS

¼ C. unsalted butter

1 T. chopped green onion

3 C. thinly sliced shiitake mushrooms

2 T. soy sauce

1 – 12 oz. steam in the bag green beans (or 3 C. fresh green beans)

DIRECTIONS

1. In a large saucepan, melt butter over medium heat.

2. Add onions, mushrooms and soy sauce. Cook 7-9 minutes, stirring occasionally.

3. Meanwhile, steam green beans according to package directions. (If you are using fresh green beans, stem and clean. Steam until fork tender.)

4. Add green beans to mushroom mixture. Stir and heat through on low heat until beans are slightly wilted, about 3 minutes.

NET CARBS 6g - per serving				
calories	fat	protein	carbs	fiber
163	12g	4g	13g	7g

Parmesan Roasted Cauliflower
with lemon caper dressing

SERVINGS: 4

Roasted and caramelized cauliflower tastes like nature's candy to me. If you are finding your roasted veggies a bit pale and flimsy, simply move the oven rack to the bottom rung where the oven will be hottest under the baking pan. Oven temp should be at least 425 degrees for most veggies.

INGREDIENTS

1 large head cauliflower

4 T. olive oil, divided

Kosher salt and black pepper, to taste

4 T. shredded parmesan cheese, divided

1 T. capers, roughly chopped

1 T. lemon juice

DIRECTIONS

1. Adjust oven rack to bottom rung and preheat oven to 450 degrees.

2. Break off green leaves of cauliflower head and core out a bit with a knife so it sits flat on a cutting surface.

3. Slice cauliflower in ½" inch slices (some florets will fall away, that's ok).

4. Line a large baking sheet with aluminum foil (not necessary but better for clean-up); arrange cauliflower on baking sheet.

5. Drizzle with 2 T. of the olive oil. Sprinkle with salt and pepper. Toss with hands to coat and rearrange in one layer as flat as possible on sheet. Bake 25-30 minutes or until deep golden brown.

6. Flip cauliflower to brown other side. Sprinkle with 2 T. parmesan cheese. Bake 10 – 12 minutes.

7. Meanwhile, to a small bowl, add the remaining oil, capers, and lemon juice. Whisk with a fork.

8. Plate cauliflower on a large platter and drizzle with lemon caper dressing; sprinkle with remaining parmesan cheese.

NET CARBS 8g - per serving				
calories	fat	protein	carbs	fiber
194	16g	5g	12g	4g

Squoodles
roasted spaghetti squash noodles

SERVINGS: 4

These squoodles (squash + noodles) are an excellent alternative to high carb pasta noodles and provide a nutty flavor. When tossed with seasonings, butter and parmesan cheese, nothing more is required to simply serve as a flavorful side dish.

INGREDIENTS

1 medium spaghetti squash

Olive oil spray, to taste

Salt and pepper, to taste

1 T. salted butter

2 T. shredded parmesan cheese

DIRECTIONS

1. Preheat oven to 400 degrees.

2. Using a large, sharp knife, slice spaghetti squash in half lengthwise; remove seeds and stringy pulp with a spoon; discard.

3. Spray interior squash flesh with olive oil; season with salt and pepper. Roast cut side down on a metal baking sheet 40 minutes.

4. Using a fork, remove squash from shells; discard shells. Place squash in a medium bowl and press with paper towels to remove as much moisture as possible or place in a cheesecloth and squeeze water out of squash noodles. (Failure to do so will result in watery squoodles.)

5. Place squoodles in a serving bowl and toss with butter and parmesan cheese. Season with additional salt and pepper, if necessary.

NET CARBS11g - per serving				
calories	fat	protein	carbs	fiber
106	6g	2g	14g	3g

Tomato Braised Cauliflower

SERVINGS: 4

The flavor that the Puttanesca Sauce brings to this fork tender cauliflower is incredibly unique and delicious. A friend of mine mentioned to me that this dish cures her craving for pasta – that's big while living the low carb lifestyle!

INGREDIENTS

1 recipe Puttanesca Sauce, pg. 124

½ C. water

1 medium head cauliflower (trim and remove large leaves)

1 T. olive oil

Chopped fresh parsley for garnish (optional)

DIRECTIONS

1. Pour the Puttanesca Sauce and water into a large saucepan; stir to mix. Bring to a low boil over medium high heat, stirring occasionally; reduce heat to medium low.

2. Place cauliflower head into the center of the sauce pan, pushing down gently. Make sure cauliflower is 1" inch from the edge of the sauce pan on all sides. Trim if necessary and place any trimmings into the sauce.

3. Pour olive oil over the top of the cauliflower.

4. Cover sauce pan and simmer 45 minutes.

5. Cauliflower will be fall-apart fork tender. To serve, slice in sauce pan and scoop out with a large spoon. Plate and drizzle with Puttanesca sauce.

6. Garnish with parsley before serving, if desired.

janeva's tips

As an alternative, you may use the Spaghizza Sauce recipe (pg. 127) in place of the Puttanesca Sauce recipe.

NET CARBS 13g - per serving				
calories	fat	protein	carbs	fiber
206	15g	6g	19g	6g

Turnip Fries
with Awesome Sauce

SERVINGS: 6

Potato fries are being kicked to the curb in the low carb lifestyle due to their higher carb content. Other veggie options are making their way to dinner plates as a great alternative. This recipe uses turnips, but you may also try using other veggies such as celery root, rutabaga, jicama and kohlrabi – the preparation is the same; only the bake time will change. It's easy enough to figure out the bake time for any veggie fry – as soon as they are golden brown on one side, just flip to the other side to brown – mark the time down for your next bake.

INGREDIENTS

fries

4 medium turnips

1 ½ T. olive or avocado oil

Greek seasoning, to taste (I use Cavender's®)

Awesome Sauce

½ C. mayonnaise

1 T. ketchup, no sugar added (I use Heinz®)

1 tsp. malt vinegar

Pinch of garlic powder

DIRECTIONS

1. Preheat oven to 425 degrees. Line a baking sheet with parchment paper.

2. Peel and cut turnips into fries — approximately 3" x ¼" inch sticks.

3. In a large bowl, toss turnip fries with oil to coat.

4. Place turnip fries in one layer on baking sheet. Sprinkle with Greek seasoning. Bake 30 minutes turning once during baking.

5. Meanwhile, make sauce by mixing all ingredients together in a bowl.

6. Serve hot turnip fries immediately with Awesome Sauce.

janeva's tips

In place of the Greek seasoning, try garlic powder, rosemary, salt and pepper, chili powder, or any other favorite seasoning(s).

NET CARBS 6g - per serving				
calories	fat	protein	carbs	fiber
191	17g	1g	8g	2g

Zoodles
spiralized zucchini noodles = Zoodles

SERVINGS: 4

Traditional pasta is pretty much impossible to fit into a low carb lifestyle due to the high carb content, so this recipe uses spiralized zucchini noodles (zoodles) as a replacement for traditional pasta noodles. You may make the zoodles yourself using a vegetable spiralizer. I use a standard hand held spiralizer which I purchased at a discount retailer; however, there are several options in the marketplace for spiralizers.

INGREDIENTS

4 medium zucchini (about 8 C. spiralized)

1 T. olive oil

1 tsp. minced garlic

Sea salt, to taste

Black pepper, to taste

DIRECTIONS

1. Cut ends off washed zucchini (no need to peel). Insert one end of zucchini into spiralizer and spiralize the zucchini into noodles (zoodles).

2. Lay several sheets of paper towels on a work surface, and spread zoodles out onto towels. Sprinkle lightly with salt. Roll up zoodles in the paper towels to absorb moisture; let rest 30 minutes.

3. Heat the oil in a large frying pan over medium/medium high heat. Add garlic and sauté 30 seconds.

4. Add zoodles and sautè 2 - 3 minutes or until cooked but still firm when bitten. Refrain from over cooking or the zoodles will turn to mush.

5. Season with sea salt and black pepper.

janeva's tips

As an alternative to making your own zoodles, they are often found pre-prepped and ready to go in your local grocer's fresh produce or freezer section.

NET CARBS 4g - per serving				
calories	fat	protein	carbs	fiber
64	4g	2g	6g	2g

Zucchini Waffle Fritters

SERVINGS: 7
(2 fritters per serving)

These savory fritters are extremely versatile and make a great snack or may be served with a bowl of soup or a dinner meal. If eating as a snack, adding a dollop of crème fraiche lightly spiked with bottled hot sauce and sprinkled with chives, hits the spot. Topping the fritters with a fried or poached egg is now a personal breakfast obsession. You will want to use a standard waffle maker, rather than a Belgian style waffle maker, to cook these fritters.

This recipe yields approximately 14 waffle fritters.

INGREDIENTS

waffle fritters

4 C. shredded zucchini

1 C. grated Vidalia onion

Salt (for draining moisture from veggies)

2 large eggs, slightly beaten

1 C. shredded parmesan cheese

1 C. shredded mozzarella cheese

Olive oil cooking spray

toppings (optional)

Crème fraiche, to taste

Bottled hot sauce, to taste

Chopped fresh chives, to taste

Poached or fried egg

DIRECTIONS

1. Lay the zucchini and onion in the middle of a kitchen towel. Sprinkle lightly with salt. Pull all 4 corners up and twist in a ball, and let rest 15 minutes.

2. Preheat waffle iron.

3. Twist kitchen towel over sink squeezing as much water out of the veggies as possible; they should feel slightly dry to the touch. This is an important step or the fritters won't cook properly.

4. Add all waffle ingredients to a medium bowl, and mix until blended.

5. Spray the hot waffle iron and scoop a heaping tablespoon into each waffle cavity; spread to about 3 inches in diameter. Bake according to manufacturers directions, approximately 2 minutes, until golden brown.

6. Cool slightly on cooling rack; serve warm. Top with optional toppings, if desired.

janeva's tips

These fritters have a very crispy cheese-like texture – if you desire a more waffle-like texture, use 3 large eggs.

NET CARBS 5g - per serving, no toppings				
calories	fat	protein	carbs	fiber
145	9g	10g	6g	1g

Desserts & Sweets

contents

Amaretti Cookies
Italian almond cookies

SERVINGS: 9

During my many travels to Italy, these cookies quickly became my favorite. They are crisp on the outside and dense and chewy on the inside. The intense almond flavor is classic and is rich tasting in this cookie. If a two-cookie serving doesn't seem enough, you will be surprised how filling and satisfying they can be!

INGREDIENTS

2 ¼ C. blanched almond flour

1 ¾ C. Splenda® granular sugar substitute

¼ tsp. baking powder

Pinch of salt

2 large egg whites

1/8 tsp. lemon juice

1 tsp. dried orange peel

1 T. almond extract

1 tsp. vanilla extract

18 whole almonds (roasted and salted)

DIRECTIONS

1. Preheat oven to 300 degrees.

2. To a large bowl, add the almond flour, Splenda, baking powder and salt. Stir with a whisk until Splenda is well incorporated into the flour. Set aside.

3. To a separate mixing bowl, add egg whites and lemon juice. Using a stand mixer or electric hand mixer, beat on high speed to stiff peaks, about two minutes. Gently fold in orange peel and extracts.

4. Add one-third dry mixture to egg white mixture; fold with a rubber spatula until mixed. Repeat until all dry ingredients are mixed with egg white mixture. Dough will be firm and sticky.

5. Using a small cookie scoop, firmly pack against bowl while scooping out; place on a parchment lined baking sheet making 18 cookies. (If a cookie scoop isn't available, roll dough into 1 ½" inch balls.)

6. Place 1 almond onto each cookie pressing down on dough to flatten cookie slightly.

7. Bake 22-24 minutes or until bottoms of cookies are lightly browned (you will have to check with a spatula as cookies don't brown on top.)

8. Cool on cooling rack. These cookies are best eaten when completely cooled; store cooled cookies in an airtight container.

janeva's tips

Splenda® should not be subbed with any other sugar substitute; this is the only brand I've found that works for these cookies.

NET CARBS 3g - per serving (2 cookies)				
calories	fat	protein	carbs	fiber
229	17g	7g	6g	3g

Angel Food Cupcakes

SERVINGS: 12
(2 cupcakes per serving)

These tender cupcakes taste like classic angel food cake and are divine topped with the Salted Caramel Frosting, pg. 260.

INGREDIENTS

2 C. blanched almond flour

¼ C. vanilla whey protein powder

2 tsp. baking powder

¼ tsp. sea salt

¼ C. + 2 T. unsalted butter, softened

½ C. Splenda® granular sugar substitute

¼ tsp. vanilla extract

2 large eggs

¼ C. heavy whipping cream

¼ C. water

Salted Caramel Frosting, pg. 260 (for topping)

DIRECTIONS

1. Preheat oven to 325 degrees.

2. Line a 24-cavity mini cupcake tin with silicone or parchment liners; set aside.

3. To a medium bowl, add almond flour, protein powder, baking powder and salt. Stir with a whisk to mix; set aside.

4. To a large mixing bowl, add butter, Splenda, and vanilla extract. Using a stand mixer or hand mixer, beat on high until blended. Add eggs one at a time until well blended.

5. Add dry ingredient mixture; blend.

6. Add heavy whipping cream and water; blend.

7. Using a small cookie scoop, scoop a level amount of batter into cupcake liners making 24 cupcakes. Bake 10-11 minutes or until an inserted toothpick comes out clean. Cool completely and frost.

janeva's tips

When frosting mini cupcakes, you will be using approximately 1 T. frosting per 2 cupcakes; add to nutrition info when using Salted Caramel Frosting recipe. The caramel drizzle in the photo is Smucker's® sugar free caramel topping.

NET CARBS 4g - per serving (no frosting)				
calories	fat	protein	carbs	fiber
194	18g	7g	6g	2g

Brandied Coffee Velvet

SERVINGS: 9
(2/3 C. serving size)

This recipe is inspired by an ice cream dessert my mom makes for an after-dinner treat. Lightly spiked for the adult crowd, brandy has 0 carbs per average serving.

When choosing a low carb ice cream, I use Breyer's® Carb Smart vanilla ice cream; the nutrition information for this recipe reflects using this brand. Blue Bunny® makes a vanilla Sweet Freedom® No Sugar Added ice cream that also works well but will change the nutrition info slightly.

INGREDIENTS

Brandied Coffee Velvet

3 T. instant coffee or espresso granules

1/3 C. warm water

1/3 C. Hershey's® sugar free chocolate syrup

¾ C. brandy

1 ½ quarts low carb vanilla ice cream, softened slightly at room temp

1 tsp. vanilla extract

toppings (optional)

Whipped cream

Lily's® stevia chocolate bar, shaved

Lily's® stevia chocolate chips

DIRECTIONS

1. In an electric stand mixing bowl, dissolve coffee granules in warm water. Add remaining ice cream ingredients.

2. Start mixing slowly using the whisk attachment; gradually increase the speed to high, and beat until smooth and thoroughly blended. Pour the mixture into a freezer safe container to store and freeze.

3. To serve, spoon into chilled dishes or glasses. Eat immediately with a spoon, or let melt a little and drink through a straw.

4. Garnish with toppings, if desired.

janeva's tips

Blending this recipe works best using a stand mixer; however, you may use an electric hand mixer (just hold on tight to the bowl with your spare hand!) Always start mixing at a slow speed until mixture is blended and then increase speed to high to blend thoroughly till you can no longer see any ice cream bits.

NET CARBS 8g - per serving (no garnishes)				
calories	fat	protein	carbs	fiber
107	5g	2g	8g	0g

desserts & sweets

Chocolate Avocado Mousse

SERVINGS: 2

For a quick and decadent chocolate fix, this mousse is a great go-to and takes only a few minutes to prep. The ripe avocado, which lends a healthy fat and a luxuriously smooth and rich texture, won't be detected in the taste.

INGREDIENTS

1 ripe avocado, peeled and pitted

¼ C. unsweetened cocoa powder

½ C. unsweetened vanilla almond milk

1 tsp. vanilla extract

1/8 tsp. salt

3 T. allulose granular sugar substitute

1/3 C. heavy cream

Whipped Cream, pg. 264, for topping (optional)

DIRECTIONS

1. Place all mousse ingredients in blender or food processor; blend on high until smooth. Refrigerate.

2. Serve chilled and topped with whipped cream, if desired.

janeva's tips

The avocado should be very ripe making a very creamy and smooth mousse; unripe avocadoes will result in lumpy bits and off-putting texture.

NET CARBS 5g - per serving no whipping cream				
calories	fat	protein	carbs	fiber
292	27g	5g	14g	9g

Chocolate Chip Cookie Cakelets

SERVINGS: 5

These little orbs of joy are packed with chocolate chips and have a soft, pillow-y and cake-like texture, yet eat like a cookie. Because I have an affinity for cake and cookies, I find these cakelets are the perfect little treat, especially when served with a cup of hot coffee or espresso!

INGREDIENTS

1 C. blanched almond flour

2 T. allulose granular sugar substitute

1/8 tsp. sea salt

1/8 tsp. baking soda

1 large egg

2 T. liquid coconut oil

1 T. almond butter

1 tsp. vanilla extract

¼ C. stevia chocolate chips (I use Lily's®)

DIRECTIONS

1. Preheat oven to 325 degrees.

2. To a medium mixing bowl, add dry ingredients (except chocolate chips). Stir with a whisk to mix.

3. Add wet ingredients. Stir to mix.

4. Fold chocolate chips into batter. Using a small cookie scoop, firmly pack against bowl while scooping; place on a parchment lined baking sheet making 10 cakelets. (If a cookie scoop isn't available, scoop dough onto baking sheet with a spoon making 1 ½" inch diameter balls.)

5. Bake 10 - 12 minutes; remove cakelets from baking pan and cool completely on cooling rack.

janeva's tips

The temptation may be to eat the cakelets hot out of the oven; however, they need to cool or they will taste dry (I know... sorry!) Let them cool completely before eating, and store in a covered container.

NET CARBS 4g - per serving				
calories	fat	protein	carbs	fiber
273	24g	7g	9g	5g

Chocolate Truffle Ice Cream Shake

SERVINGS: 2

You will need to make the Flourless Chocolate Truffle Cake on pg. 246 to make this shake. Please note that this dessert is a super special treat that should be enjoyed only on occasion as the calories and carbs are slightly higher in comparison to the average low carb sweet treat. I believe that life is a balance and we should indulge once in a while in something that is decadent.

After creating the truffle cake recipe, I found that it was so rich that only a small slice is required to feel satisfied; so, what was I going to do with the remaining cake? I froze the cake in individual slices and thought these would make a good chocolate ice cream base. So here you are with a bonus recipe for leftover cake and a super indulgent ice cream shake that is incredible in texture and taste.

INGREDIENTS

1 slice (serving) Flourless Chocolate Truffle Cake, pg. 246

1 ½ C. ice cubes

½ C. unsweetened vanilla almond milk

¼ C. heavy whipping cream

DIRECTIONS

1. Place all ingredients in a blender and blend until smooth and creamy.

NET CARBS 14g - per serving, no toppings				
calories	fat	protein	carbs	fiber
370	34g	6g	24g	10g

Cream Cheese Glaze

SERVINGS: 12
(1 T. serving size)

I find the standard glaze texture to be too thin and too sweet. For this recipe, I've created a fluffier version that complements denser textured, low carb baked goods. This recipe provides a perfectly light and fluffy glaze that has the rich, tangy flavor of cream cheese.

INGREDIENTS

3 oz. cream cheese, softened

3 T. erythritol confectioners sugar (I use Swerve®)

1 tsp. clear vanilla extract

¼ C. heavy whipping cream

DIRECTIONS

1. Place cream cheese, confectioners sugar and extract in a small mixing bowl. Using an electric hand mixer, beat until creamy.

2. Slowly add heavy whipping cream while mixing. Mix just until smooth and creamy. Store in a covered container in fridge.

janeva's tips

To drizzle glaze over baked goods, fill a sandwich size plastic bag with glaze. Cut a small piece off the corner of the bag, and squeeze bag to drizzle glaze over baked goods.

NET CARBS 1g - per serving				
calories	fat	protein	carbs	fiber
43	4g	1g	1g	0g

Crème Brulee

SERVINGS: 4

INGREDIENTS

6 large egg yolks

¼ C. Swerve® granular sugar substitute

1 ½ C. heavy whipping cream

¾ tsp. pure vanilla extract

4 tsp. sugar, divided (for topping)

janeva's tips

Oven broiler method for caramelizing sugar (brulee) — evenly sprinkle sugar over chilled crème brulees and set ramekins on a baking sheet. Place ramekins no more than 5" inches under oven broiler. Broil until sugar melts and caramelizes, approximately 2 minutes or less, watching closely to prevent burning! Remove ramekins from oven and let rest 5 minutes until sugar has hardened.

DIRECTIONS

1. Preheat oven to 300 degrees.

2. To a medium bowl, add egg yolks and granular sugar substitute. Using an electric hand mixer, blend on high 2 ½ - 3 minutes, or until thick and light in color.

3. Add heavy cream and vanilla extract to yolk mixture. Blend on low speed 30 seconds until mixed. Strain mixture through a metal sieve into a large bowl; skim off any foam or bubbles.

4. Evenly pour crème brulee mixture into four ramekins (3 ¼" diameter x 1 ¾" inch high); set ramekins in an 8" x 8" inch square baking dish. Fill baking dish with hot tap water until halfway up ramekins.

5. Carefully move baking dish into oven making sure not to get any water into ramekins. Bake approximately 50-55 minutes or until crème brulee edges are set, but still slightly loose in center.

6. Remove pan from oven, and let cool on wire rack. Remove ramekins from pan, cover with plastic wrap, and place in fridge at least 2 hours to chill.

7. Just before serving, sprinkle 1 tsp. sugar evenly over each custard. Using a culinary torch, move torch back and forth over the surface of the sugar to brown and caramelize. Let rest 5 minutes to allow caramel to harden before eating. If you do not own a culinary torch, see TIP for alternative method for caramelizing sugar.

NET CARBS 8g - per serving				
calories	fat	protein	carbs	fiber
409	40g	6g	8g	0g

desserts & sweets

Crème brulee is my all-time favorite dessert, and I knew I had to create a low carb version. This version far exceeded my expectations! For years I put off making crème brulee because I thought it would require a skill set that I wasn't familiar with, plus it has a name that sounds unattainably fancy -- but I'm here to say, try it, no matter your skill set! Just follow the recipe to a 'T' and you may surprise yourself. This is the only recipe I have in this cookbook that requires real sugar. Real sugar? Yes, the real sugar is necessary for the caramelized topping that hardens and cracks when using a spoon and provides part of the fun while eating this dessert. Since I don't stock real sugar in my pantry, I pick up a few packets when ordering coffee at my favorite coffee shop and tote them home with me. The amount of net carbs per serving of this dessert is just 8 grams per serving. Score!

There are a few more points to mention here before you let loose in the kitchen to attempt this French dessert. The size of the ramekins is important or they won't cook or set correctly; the size is listed in the recipe directions. In order to create a good brulee, I highly recommend purchasing a culinary torch; however, an alternative method for caramelizing the sugar is listed in the TIP section using a standard oven broiler.

Channel your inner French chef and go for it!

Flourless Chocolate Truffle Cake

SERVINGS: 16

INGREDIENTS

cake

½ C. water

¼ tsp. sea salt

¾ C. allulose granular sugar substitute

18 oz. (2 pkg.) stevia chocolate chips (I use Lily's®)

1 C. (2 sticks) salted butter

1 tsp. instant espresso powder

1 tsp. vanilla extract

6 eggs

Cooking spray

toppings (optional)

Cocoa powder, for dusting

Whipped cream, pg. 264

Berries of choice

DIRECTIONS

1. Preheat oven to 300 degrees.

2. Prepare an 8" inch round glass cakepan by spraying with cooking spray. Cut an 8" inch circle of parchment paper and line the bottom; spray top of parchment. Set aside.

3. In a small sauce pan, add water, sea salt and allulose. Heat over medium heat a few minutes; stir until allulose is dissolved and water is clear. Set aside.

4. Place the chocolate chips in a medium size microwave proof bowl. Cut butter into pieces and fold into chocolate chips.

5. Microwave 1 ½ minutes on high; stir. Microwave ½ minute more; stir.

6. Pour chocolate mixture into an electric stand mixer bowl. Add espresso powder and vanilla; mix on slow speed until blended and turn to medium-high speed until batter is smooth.

7. While mixing, slowly pour water mixture into chocolate batter until smooth.

8. Add one egg at a time and mix until smooth.

9. Pour batter into cake pan and set cake pan into a larger pan (a 9" x 13" inch casserole works well); pour enough boiling water into the larger pan until it reaches halfway up sides of cake pan.

10. Carefully place in oven; be careful not to get water into cake batter.

11. Bake 45 minutes. Cake will look wet in the middle, the edges baked. Remove cake pan from water bath. Cool completely on a cooling rack; cover and place in the refrigerator overnight.

12. To serve, run a knife around the edge of the cake to loosen; place a plate upside down on top of pan and turn over. To cut, heat a sharp knife under hot running water, slice and clean; do this with each cut.

13. Dust with cocoa powder and top with whipped cream and fresh berries, if desired. Keep refrigerated.

NET CARBS 13g - per serving (no toppings)				
calories	fat	protein	carbs	fiber
259	22g	5g	23g	10g

This decadent cake eats more like a rich chocolate truffle than a cake. My first thought after creating this recipe was, 'How is all this cake going to be eaten when a small sliver is all one needs?' I'm happy to report that this cake freezes well when wrapped tightly in plastic wrap in single size servings. When needing a chocolate fix, it's the perfect solution. I've also created a bonus Chocolate Truffle Ice Cream Shake using slices of this cake. Check it out on pg. 240 in this cookbook. It's incredible!

Jitterbug Ice Cream
jitter = coffee beans | bug(s) = chocolate chips

SERVINGS: 6

(1/2 C. servings)
Recipe makes 3 C. ice cream.

There is just a 'hint' of coffee flavor in this ice cream that lends a delicate taste to the vanilla base. If you don't want to steep the ice cream base in the coffee beans, skip steps referring to coffee beans in the directions; essentially you will end up with vanilla chocolate chip ice cream – no complaints there! I hope you like rich, silky, creamy, custard-like ice cream? If so, this recipe is perfect for you!

INGREDIENTS

2 C. heavy whipping cream

½ C. unsweetened almond milk, plain or vanilla

¼ C. whole coffee beans

¼ C. allulose granular sugar substitute

2 pinches sea salt

4 large egg yolks

¼ tsp. xanthan gum

1/3 C. stevia chocolate chips (I use Lily's®)

janeva's tips

You may never regret investing in a good ice cream maker! This ice cream is the best I've ever had, and with the absence of guilt, eating this sugar free version makes it even better. If an electric ice cream maker is not available, use this alternative method -- pour ice cream mixture into ice cube trays and freeze. When ready to eat, place ice cream cubes in a blender; blend until creamy; stir in chocolate chips.

DIRECTIONS

1. To a medium microwave-proof bowl, add heavy cream, almond milk and coffee beans; stir. To steep coffee flavor into cream base, cover and place in fridge for 4 hours or overnight.

2. Heat ice cream base in microwave on high for 2 minutes; stir. Strain to remove coffee beans; discard beans. Return ice cream base back into bowl.

3. Add allulose and sea salt to ice cream base; stir to mix. Add egg yolks one at a time while stirring, until each yolk is well mixed into ice cream base. Continue stirring while adding xanthan gum; stir until mixed.

4. Heat ice cream base on high in microwave for 2 minutes, stirring every 30 seconds, until thickened. Cool ice cream in fridge or 20-30 minutes in freezer and place in an electric ice cream maker; churn ice cream according to manufacturer directions, adding chocolate chips toward end of churning. (If you don't have an ice cream maker, see TIP.)

5. Best if eaten immediately but may easily be stored in freezer. To serve, remove ice cream and let rest at room temp to thaw a bit before scooping.

NET CARBS 5g - per serving				
calories	fat	protein	carbs	fiber
336	34g	4g	10g	5g

Lemon Supreme Pound Cake

SERVINGS: 12

This lemon supreme pound cake has been perfected to be light, buttery and full of fresh lemon flavor. I like serving this pound cake sliced and spread with salted butter, topped with whipped cream and berries, or spread with the Cream Cheese Glaze, pg. 242.

INGREDIENTS

2 C. blanched almond flour

1 T. Bob's Red Mill® vital wheat gluten

½ tsp. salt

½ C. (1 stick) unsalted butter, softened

5 oz. cream cheese, softened

¾ C. allulose granular sugar substitute

4 large eggs, room temp

Zest of one lemon

janeva's tips

It is important to note that the ingredients should be room temp as cold ingredients may cause the loaf to sink. The vital wheat gluten provides structure to the cake, so it won't crumble and fall apart after slicing. For those who may be celiac or gluten sensitive, the vital wheat gluten may be omitted but will slightly change the texture of the cake.

DIRECTIONS

1. Preheat oven to 325 degrees.

2. Line a standard 9" x 5" inch loaf pan with parchment paper allowing paper to hang over sides (this will make it easier to lift out when cooled); set prepared pan aside.

3. To a medium bowl, add dry ingredients. Stir with whisk 30 seconds to mix; set aside.

4. To a large mixing bowl, add butter, cream cheese and allulose. Using a stand mixer or electric hand mixer, beat on high until creamy (about 30 seconds.) Add eggs one at a time, mixing on medium low speed just until each egg is mixed into batter. Refrain from over beating.

5. Slowly add dry ingredients to wet ingredients, mixing on low speed just until blended.

6. Add lemon zest to batter; fold to mix.

7. Pour batter into loaf pan. Level batter with a spatula.

8. Bake 45 minutes. Loosely cover pound cake with a sheet of aluminum foil by tenting over the top of the loaf pan. (Cake may become dark golden brown on the outside; that's normal — the aluminum foil will prevent further browning before cake is baked through.) Bake an additional 15-20 minutes, or until an inserted toothpick comes clean.

9. Transfer pan to cooling rack and cool completely. Store in fridge.

NET CARBS 7g - per serving (no toppings)				
calories	fat	protein	carbs	fiber
242	20g	9g	8g	1g

Mini Fruit Cheesecakes

SERVINGS: 2

Cheesecake is not only a perfect bite for a sweet tooth but a perfect low carb dessert with only 1 gram net carb per serving for each of these mini versions. They freeze and thaw well, so making them in batches is a great way to always have them ready for a special treat. The cheesecakes may be eaten plain but the fruit jam, syrup and berries amp the flavor — they're eye candy too!

INGREDIENTS

crust

1/3 C. whole pecans, unsalted

1/3 C. blanched almond flour

2 T. unsalted butter, melted

Cooking spray or parchment baking liners

filling

8 oz. cream cheese, room temperature

1/3 C. allulose granular sugar substitute

1 tsp. vanilla extract

1 tsp. lemon juice

1 egg

toppings (optional)

Sugar free fruit jams

Sugar free strawberry ice cream syrup

Assorted fresh berries

DIRECTIONS

1. Preheat oven to 350 degrees.

2. In a food processor, pulse pecans to crumbs and transfer to a small mixing bowl. Add almond flour and melted butter; stir with a fork until mixed.

3. Using your fingers and/or the back of a spoon, press crumb mixture firmly into a sprayed muffin tin (12 cavity), making 9 cheesecake crusts. Bake 5 minutes; cool in pan on cooling rack while preparing cheesecake filling.

4. To a medium bowl, add all filling ingredients except egg. Blend with an electric hand mixer until creamy. Add egg and blend just until smooth (don't over mix.)

5. Evenly pour cheesecake mixture over pre-baked crusts. Bake 13-15 minutes or until middles are set.

6. Cool in pan on a cooling rack. Cover and refrigerate in pan one hour or more before eating.

7. Run a knife around cheesecakes to remove from pan (if not using liners). Plate and top with optional toppings. Store refrigerated.

NET CARBS 1g - per serving (no toppings)				
calories	fat	protein	carbs	fiber
176	16g	4g	6g	5g

Peanut Butter Angel Cookies

Time for a quick story and testimony to this recipe! During a telephone conversation with a friend from West Virginia and an invite to visit him, I mentioned that I was in the middle of making sugar free peanut butter cookies and he replied, "They sound awful!" I reassured him that they were incredible and that I would make him a batch and bring them along on my trip.

My early flight started in Minneapolis where we were held up on the tarmac for nearly an hour before take-off. Sitting next to a United Airlines employee, we began to chat. Neither of us had eaten breakfast before our flight, so with a growling stomach I brought out the Peanut Butter Angel Cookies from my carry-on to share with him. He thought they were spectacular and mentioned that his diabetic wife would also likely love them. Off we went to our separate destinations and soon I landed in West Virginia.

Making a fresh batch for my friend, he took them to work for his employees and they were gobbled up in minutes. Score! After a week passed, it was time to fly home. Upon checking in at the United Airlines counter, the service agent took my credentials and giggled as she viewed the computer screen. We were puzzled, what was so funny? She excused herself to retrieve her manager and he also giggled after viewing the screen. He looked up at me and asked, "Do you have a killer cookie recipe? One of our United Airline employees put a note in your file asking for your recipe upon check-in. Here is his phone number. He'd appreciate it if you could text the cookie recipe to him. He wants to make them as a surprise treat for his wife."

I hope you enjoy them equally as much!

SERVINGS: 16 (1 cookie)

INGREDIENTS

1 C. creamy natural peanut butter, no added sugar

1 ¼ C. Splenda® granular sugar substitute

1 large egg

1 tsp. vanilla extract

janeva's tips

Splenda® must be used in this recipe; other sugar substitutes will not work.

DIRECTIONS

1. Preheat oven to 350 degrees.

2. Line a baking sheet with parchment paper; set aside.

3. Place ¼ C. Splenda into a bowl for coating the cookies; set aside.

4. To a medium mixing bowl, add peanut butter, 1 C. Splenda®, egg and vanilla. Using an electric hand mixer, mix until smooth and blended.

5. Using a small cookie scoop or tablespoon, scoop batter and roll into a ball between hands making 16 cookies; roll cookie balls in Splenda® to coat, and place on baking sheet 2" apart.

6. Using a fork, press down on each cookie making a criss-cross pattern.

7. Bake 12 - 14 minutes or until lightly browned.

8. Let cool on baking sheet a few minutes before removing to cooling rack.

NET CARBS 2g - per serving				
calories	fat	protein	carbs	fiber
100	8g	4g	3g	1g

Pistachio Fluff

SERVINGS: 8

When I was growing up, my mom made a dessert named 'Next Best Thing to Robert Redford' — it had a nutty, flaky crust that was layered with a cream cheese filling, pistachio pudding and topped with whipped cream. I adored this dessert and set out to make 'The Next Best Thing to Her Dessert.' The crust is tricky to make low carb, so instead I created the same flavors using a few simple ingredients. My version tastes every bit as good as her recipe — the best part is eating it guilt free!

INGREDIENTS

8 oz. cream cheese, softened

1 C. cold water

1 C. heavy cream

1 pkg. (1 oz) Jello® sugar free pistachio instant pudding

1 C. salted mixed nuts, coarsely chopped*

Whipped cream, pg. 264, for topping (optional)

DIRECTIONS

1. Add cream cheese, water and whipping cream to a large bowl. Using an electric hand mixer or stand mixer, beat on medium high speed until blended.

2. Add dry pudding and beat on high speed setting 1-2 minutes or until light and fluffy to texture of your liking.

3. Layer pistachio mixture alternately with chopped nuts in a parfait style glass, or scoop into a dessert bowl and sprinkle with nuts. Top with whipped cream, if desired. Serve chilled.

janeva's tips

*Chopped nuts should not include peanuts as they will overpower the flavor of the dish; this dessert is best with a combination of pecans, almonds, Brazil nuts, walnuts and macadamia nuts. You may use another pudding flavor in place of the pistachio pudding.

NET CARBS 3g - per serving (no whipped topping)				
calories	fat	protein	carbs	fiber
294	28g	6g	5g	2g

Rhuberry Compote

The definition of compote is simply just cooked fruit. This recipe was inspired by my mom's rhubarb cream pie and her fruit compote served every Christmas as a side dish. I've combined the two inspirations to make this dessert using rhubarb and berries, hence Rhuberry. While rhubarb is classified as a vegetable, it cooks like a fruit. Here in Minnesota, fresh rhubarb bushes grow like wildflowers in the yards of many neighborhoods. Requiring a hard frost for growth, rhubarb is very common in the northern regions of North America. For those in the southern regions, it is challenging to find it at your local grocers. If you are unable to find rhubarb, simply use all berries, or plead with your friends in the north to ship some to you.

The combination of the tart and sweet makes this compote versatile for serving over ice cream, yogurt, pancakes and waffles, adding to smoothies, blending and using as jam, or drizzled with heavy cream as stated in this recipe for a perfectly sweet, tart and creamy dessert!

SERVINGS: 6

INGREDIENTS

compote

1 ½ C. chopped fresh or frozen rhubarb (cut in ½" chunks)

1 ½ C. frozen mixed berries (blackberries, raspberries and blueberries)

1 ¼ C. allulose granular sugar substitute

1 tsp. glucomannan powder (konjac powder)

Dash of salt

2 large eggs, beaten

1 T. unsalted butter, melted

toppings

¾ C. heavy whipping cream

Toasted pecans, to taste (optional)*

DIRECTIONS

1. Preheat oven to 450 degrees.

2. In an 8" x 8" inch square baking dish, evenly spread rhubarb and berries in bottom of pan; set aside.

3. In a medium bowl, add the allulose, glucomannan and salt. Stir with a whisk to mix.

4. In a separate bowl, slowly add melted butter to beaten eggs, stirring constantly until mixed.

5. Add egg mixture to dry mixture. Using a hand held electric beater, beat until creamy and pour over rhuberry mixture.

6. Cover pan with aluminum foil and bake 10 minutes at 450 degrees. Lower oven heat to 350 degrees, and bake 35 minutes. Turn off oven and bake an additional 15 minutes. Cool on cooling rack.

7. Serve warmed, room temp, or chilled in small bowls and evenly drizzle heavy whipping cream over each serving. Sprinkle with chopped toasted pecans, if desired.

janeva's tips

*To toast pecans, heat a dry frying pan over medium heat. Add whole pecans and stir constantly, about 1-2 minutes, until fragrant and toasted. Immediately remove from heat, chop, and sprinkle on dessert.

NET CARBS 4g - per serving (no pecans)				
calories	fat	protein	carbs	fiber
194	15g	3g	6g	2g

Salted Caramel Frosting

SERVINGS: 14
(1 T. serving size)

The classic flavor of salted caramel in this frosting is lightly sweet with a bit of tang from the cream cheese and just a hint of sea salt -- the perfect balance of flavors for an incredible tasting frosting.

INGREDIENTS

¼ c. unsalted butter, softened

4 oz. cream cheese, softened

2 T. sugar free caramel topping (I use Smuckers®)

1 T. confectioners sugar substitute (I use Swerve®)

Flake sea salt, to taste (for topping)

DIRECTIONS

1. To a small mixing bowl, add butter, cream cheese, caramel topping and confectioners sugar. Whisk until blended and creamy.

2. Frost baked goods and sprinkle with flake sea salt. Drizzle with additional caramel topping, if desired.

NET CARBS 1g - per serving				
calories	fat	protein	carbs	fiber
64	6g	1g	1g	0g

desserts & sweets

Strawberry Shortcake

Thankfully, strawberries are one of the lower carb fruits. As a child, I remember two different versions for shortcake. One was more cake-like and the kind you might see pre-packaged and sold in a grocery store. The other, a made-from-scratch sweet biscuit — those are the kind I loved. These shortcakes were created from those memories.

INGREDIENTS

shortcake

1 C. blanched almond flour

2 T. coconut flour

2 T. allulose granular sugar substitute

1 ½ tsp. baking powder

1/8 tsp. salt

1 large egg

1 T. sour cream

1 T. heavy whipping cream

½ tsp. vanilla extract

toppings

1 ½ C. fresh strawberries, sliced or quartered

¾ C. Whipped Cream, pg. 264

BochaSweet® granular sugar substitute, to taste (or other favorite brand)*

Sugar free strawberry ice cream topping (I use Smuckers®), optional

DIRECTIONS

1. Preheat oven to 325 degrees.

2. In a medium mixing bowl, add dry shortcake ingredients and stir with a whisk to mix.

3. Add remaining shortcake ingredients. Stir to mix or use a hand held electric mixer to blend.

4. Separate dough into 6 equal pieces. Hand form each piece into round shortcakes 2 ¼" inches in diameter. Place shortcakes onto a parchment lined baking sheet.

5. Bake 15 – 17 minutes or until light golden brown; remove shortcakes from baking sheet and cool on cooling rack.

6. To assemble, carefully slice shortcakes in half horizontally. Plate shortcake bottoms and evenly top with strawberries, whipped cream, and sprinkle with BochaSweet®. Top with remaining shortcake halves and drizzle with strawberry topping, if desired.

janeva's tips

*I use BochaSweet® granular to top this dessert because it's shimmering and beautiful, making a stunning presentation; however, you may use any brand granular sugar substitute in its place. Shortcakes may be frozen for another time.

NET CARBS 7g - per serving				
calories	fat	protein	carbs	fiber
217	14g	6g	13g	6g

Whipped Cream

SERVINGS: 16
(2 T. serving size)

A rich and creamy topping, perfect for any dessert. Delicious served as a topping for a hot cup of coffee or hot chocolate or simply eat by the spoonful at times of sweet cravings. The vanilla flavor may be changed by adding 1/4 tsp cinnamon, pumpkin or apple spice, or sub the vanilla extract for other flavors. Make it your own favorite flavored whipped cream!

INGREDIENTS

1 C. heavy whipping cream

1 tsp. confectioners sugar substitute (I use Swerve®)

1 tsp. clear vanilla extract

DIRECTIONS

1. Place a medium metal or glass mixing bowl in the freezer for 10 minutes to chill.

2. Remove bowl and add heavy whipping cream.

3. Using an electric hand mixer, beat on high while slowly adding remaining ingredients.

4. Beat to stiff peaks. Taste and adjust sugar substitute to your liking, if necessary. Store covered in fridge until ready to use. Whipped cream lasts approximately 2-3 days in fridge.

janeva's tips

Beat just until peaks are stiff or you will end up with butter. To test for stiff peaks, turn off mixer and pull beaters straight up out of whipped cream; if the peaks stand up straight and don't fall, you have stiff peaks. Recipe makes 2 C. whipped cream.

NET CARBS 1g - per serving				
calories	fat	protein	carbs	fiber
52	6g	1g	1g	0g

White Chocolate Berry Parfaits

SERVINGS: 6

This is an indulgent dessert that is whipped up in a few minutes and will surely impress family, friends – and yourself! The rich cream cheese, sweet white chocolate, and tart berries is a combination that will satisfy any dessert lover.

INGREDIENTS

8 oz. cream cheese, softened (room temp)

1 pkg. (1 oz.) Jell-O® white chocolate instant pudding, sugar free

1 C. heavy cream

1 C. cold water

1 C. sliced strawberries, raspberries or blueberries (or combination)

DIRECTIONS

1. Add cream cheese, water and whipping cream to a large bowl. Using an electric hand mixer or stand mixer, beat on medium high speed until blended.

2. Add instant pudding; beat on high speed setting until light and fluffy to texture of your liking.

3. Layer pudding mixture alternately with berries in a parfait style glass. Serve chilled.

NET CARBS 8g - per serving				
calories	fat	protein	carbs	fiber
297	27g	4g	9g	1g

Zucchini Bread Popsicles

SERVINGS: 6 popsicles
(Servings may change based on popsicle mold size.)

Yes, you read that right – Zucchini Bread Popsicles. No, there is not zucchini bread in these ice cream popsicles; however, the ingredients make the popsicles taste like zucchini bread! Curious? Give these a try — they're easy to make and a fantastic treat!

INGREDIENTS

popsicles

1 medium zucchini

½ C. old fashioned oats

1 ½ C. unsweetened vanilla cashew or almond milk (I use Silk®)

2/3 C. allulose granular sugar substitute

1 tsp. vanilla extract

1/8 tsp. cinnamon

14 oz. can coconut milk (I use Thai Kitchen®)

mix-ins (optional)

2 T. chopped walnuts or pecans

2 T. stevia chocolate chips (I use Lily's®)

DIRECTIONS

1. Cut ends off zucchini (no need to peel.) Cut zucchini in half lengthwise. Run a spoon down the center of each half and scoop out pulp; discard. Finely shred zucchini using a hand grater or food processor.

2. To a medium saucepan, add shredded zucchini, oats, cashew milk, allulose, vanilla and cinnamon. Stir to mix. Heat over medium/medium high heat, stirring often, for 7- 9 minutes or until oats are cooked and mixture is thickened.

3. Remove from heat and stir in coconut milk until blended; cool in freezer 15 minutes (if using mix-ins the mixture will need to cool; if not, no need to cool and the mixture can be poured directly into popsicle molds.) Stir mix-ins into cooled popsicle mixture, if desired.

4. Pour mixture into popsicle molds and freeze.

janeva's tips

As a fun alternative to making the popsicles, I like to pour the mixture into ice cube trays and stick a toothpick in each cube and freeze. These make excellent little snacks when you're looking to satisfy a sweet tooth without wanting to eat an entire popsicle. Nutrition info will need to be adjusted to reflect the smaller snack size.

NET CARBS 7g - per serving (no mix-ins)				
calories	fat	protein	carbs	fiber
155	12g	1g	8g	1g

Snacks & Miscellaneous

contents

Antipasto

SERVINGS: 18
(1/2 C. servings)

After first starting the low carb lifestyle, I quickly learned that meat sticks and cheese were a good snack choice, yet that became a bit of a yawn-fest over time. I wanted something more, something flavorful. Antipasto translates to the traditional first course of an Italian meal; however, I prep this in a big bowl on Sunday and eat for a snack the entire week. As an option, serve on a bed of lettuce as a filling salad and lunch idea, or double (or triple) the recipe and serve at a party or gathering.

INGREDIENTS

8 oz. block cheddar cheese, cut in cubes

8 oz. block provolone cheese, cut in cubes

8 oz. hard salami, cut in bite size pieces

½ C. mini pepperoni slices

2.25 oz. can sliced black olives, drained

14 oz. can artichokes, drained and chopped

2 green onions, chopped

1 green pepper, chopped

½ jalapeno, chopped (seeds and membrane removed)

2 T. Italian dressing or other favorite low carb salad dressing, optional

DIRECTIONS

1. To a large bowl, add antipasto ingredients. Gently fold to mix.

2. Drizzle dressing over top and fold, if using. Store refrigerated.

janeva's tips

Nutrition info will vary based on brands purchased for use in this recipe; the included nutrition info is an estimate only. I like this snack without salad dressing but it may be added for extra flavor, if desired. Recipe makes approximately 9 C. antipasto.

NET CARBS 2g - per serving (no dressing)				
calories	fat	protein	carbs	fiber
174	14g	10g	2g	0g

BLT
Spears

SERVINGS: 2
(2 spears serving size)

Bacon, lettuce and tomato sandwiches remind me of summertime in Minnesota. I always look forward to ripe, garden-fresh tomatoes sold at farmers markets -- a perfect addition to a great BLT sandwich. In this version, I've created a low carb breadless version simply by layering the ingredients in a romaine lettuce leaf. Buh-bye bread, you're not needed in this delicious recipe! These BLT Spears make an excellent snack or light lunch.

INGREDIENTS

4 slices thick cut bacon

4 whole romaine leaves

2 T. mayonnaise

12 grape or baby heirloom tomatoes, halved

Freshly ground black pepper, to taste

DIRECTIONS

1. Preheat oven to 400 degrees.

2. Line a baking sheet with aluminum foil. Lay bacon on foil in a single layer.

3. Bake 15 minutes or until browned and crispy. Transfer bacon to a paper towel lined plate to drain, and discard bacon grease.

4. Evenly spread mayonnaise on each of the romaine leaves; layer evenly with tomato halves, black pepper and bacon slices. Fold romaine leaf in half lengthwise to cradle bacon and tomatoes.

NET CARBS 4g - per serving				
calories	fat	protein	carbs	fiber
259	21g	10g	9g	5g

Buffalo Chicken Stuffed Celery

SERVINGS: 20

This is a perfect snack for game day (or any day) and is versatile enough to keep in the fridge for personal snacking or bring to a gathering. As an alternative, try stuffing in mini sweet bell peppers or top cucumber slices with dip — dip may be served hot or cold.

INGREDIENTS

buffalo dip

2 C. cooked shredded chicken

8 oz. cream cheese, softened

½ C. ranch dressing

½ C. shredded mozzarella cheese

¼ C. buffalo wing sauce (I use Franks®)

20 celery stalks

toppings (optional)

Chopped green onion, to taste

Buffalo wing sauce, to taste

DIRECTIONS

1. Place all dip ingredients (except celery) in a medium mixing bowl.

2. Mix with an electric hand mixer until blended.

3. Fill celery stalks and cut in serving size pieces.

4. Plate and drizzle with additional buffalo wing sauce and green onions, if desired. Keep dip refrigerated.

janeva's tips

Instead of stuffing the celery, you may serve the dip in a bowl with the celery on the side for dipping. To heat dip and serve hot, microwave on medium-high power to desired temperature; stir before serving.

NET CARBS 1g - per serving (no toppings)				
calories	fat	protein	carbs	fiber
98	8g	4g	1g	0g

Caramel Apple Jicama Stix

SERVINGS: 4

This recipe has truly been a game changer for guilt free snacking. The stix are easy to make and portable to take with you on-the-go. We make and take them on our boat on hot sunny days, keeping them in our cooler — a perfect low carb and refreshing snack. Kids love them too!

INGREDIENTS

3 C. jicama stix (peel jicama and cut the size of fries)

1 T. olive oil

1 T. + 2 tsp. apple cider vinegar

2 T. sugar free caramel syrup (I use Smucker's®)

1 T. sugar free maple syrup

1 tsp. cinnamon

2 pinches salt

DIRECTIONS

1. Place jicama stix in a large bowl and set aside.

2. In a medium bowl, whisk the remaining ingredients.

3. Pour the caramel mixture over the jicama stix, and toss to coat.

4. Cover and keep refrigerated.

janeva's tips

Marinate jicama stix in the caramel mixture in fridge for 2-4 hours for best flavor. Toss to coat before serving.

NET CARBS 4g - per serving				
calories	fat	protein	carbs	fiber
68	3g	1g	9g	5g

Cauliflower Pizza Crust

SERVINGS: 2

Never thought I'd like pizza crust made with a vegetable but this recipe for a crust is excellent and I now prefer it over the high carb flour crusts. Sure, it would be easier to pull a frozen pizza out of the freezer, but the reality is this takes 15 minutes to assemble and is well worth the effort!

Because toppings will vary by personal preference, this recipe is for the crust only – check out how to assemble it to a finished pizza in the assembly directions below.

INGREDIENTS

crust only

4 C. cauliflower florets

1 C. water

1 tsp. Italian seasoning

1 tsp. garlic powder

½ tsp. crushed red pepper

¼ C. shredded parmesan cheese

½ C. shredded mozzarella cheese

1 large egg, slightly beaten

assembly

For the pizza sauce, I use the Spaghizza sauce, pg. 127; or, you may use your own favorite low carb pizza sauce. To assemble, I like to top with a variety of cooked meat and/or veggies, drizzle with warmed pizza sauce, and sprinkle with shredded cheese. This assembly helps to prevent the crust from becoming limp from the sauce. Place the pizza back in the oven and bake at 400 degrees or broil until cheese is melted and pizza is heated through.

DIRECTIONS

1. Preheat oven to 400 degrees.

2. Place cauliflower in a microwave proof bowl; add water. Cover and cook on high 12 minutes or until fork tender; drain.

3. Place semi-cooled cauliflower in a kitchen towel; twist the towel to make a ball and squeeze as much water out as possible until the cauliflower is 'dry'. (Do not rush this step or the crust won't cook properly.)

4. Place the cauliflower in a large bowl and add remaining ingredients; mix until well blended.

5. Line a work surface with parchment paper. Place cauliflower mixture in the center and put another piece of parchment paper on top. Roll or press into a 10" inch diameter circle. Remove parchment paper from top of crust. Keep crust on remaining parchment paper, and transfer to a baking sheet.

6. Bake 20 minutes or until light golden brown. Using the edge of the parchment paper, flip pizza over onto baking sheet; toss parchment paper.

7. Turn off oven and bake another 5 – 7 minutes. Cool on cooling rack and top with your favorite toppings. See assembly.

NET CARBS 8g - per serving (crust only)				
calories	fat	protein	carbs	fiber
231	13g	17g	14g	6g

Cheese Crisps

SERVINGS: 4

Move over potato chips, these crispy crunchy snacks are low carb and perfect for snacking. Cheese crisps are so simple and easy to make that they really don't need a recipe; however, if I don't make them for a while, I forget the measurements, time and temp so I like to have the recipe handy. I like them plain, but you may add a light sprinkle of your favorite seasoning(s) on top before baking.

INGREDIENTS

1 ½ C. shredded fresh parmesan cheese

Dried Italian seasoning or other favorite seasoning, to taste (optional)

DIRECTIONS

1. Preheat oven to 400 degrees.

2. Scoop cheese by heaping tablespoon onto a parchment lined baking sheet. Evenly pat down cheese into a 3-inch round. Sprinkle with seasoning(s), if desired.

3. Repeat with remaining cheese spacing crisps 1" inch apart yielding approximately 24 – 30 crisps. (This will need to be done in batches.)

4. Bake 3 – 5 minutes or until lightly browned and crisp. Remove from oven, and let cool on baking sheet one minute; transfer to a cooling rack.

NET CARBS 2g - per serving				
calories	fat	protein	carbs	fiber
165	12g	14g	2g	0g

Crispy Hot Wings
with creamy blue cheese dip

SERVINGS: 6

Crispy on the outside, tender on the inside -- every time I make these chicken wings I think about them for days. That's the kind of recipe worthy of sharing in a cookbook.

INGREDIENTS

wings

2 lbs. chicken wings

marinade

¼ C. Buffalo hot sauce (I use Franks®)

3 T. salted butter, melted

1 tsp. Hungarian paprika

½ tsp. salt

¼ tsp. black pepper

creamy blue cheese dip

½ C. crumbled blue cheese

½ C. sour cream

½ C. mayonnaise

1 tsp. white vinegar

¼ tsp. garlic powder

DIRECTIONS

1. Cut and discard wing tips from chicken wings. Cut wings at the joint and place in a large bowl. Set aside.

2. In a medium bowl, mix marinade. Remove 2 T. of prepared marinade to a separate bowl; set aside. You will use this later.

3. Pour the remaining marinade over chicken wings, and toss to coat. Cover and refrigerate ½ hour, to marinate.

4. Meanwhile, make blue cheese dip by placing all ingredients in a blender. Blend on high until creamy. Store covered in fridge until ready to use.

5. Turn on oven broiler. Place wings on a baking sheet spaced 1-2" apart. Broil wings 4-5" from broiler for 8-10 minutes. Turn wings over and broil another 8-10 minutes.

6. Add cooked wings to a large, clean bowl. Pour the 2 T. reserved marinade over wings and toss to coat.

7. Serve hot with blue cheese dip.

janeva's tips

If you're into hot and spicy, add ¼ - ½ tsp. cayenne pepper to the marinade. Wings are great served with celery sticks. Blue cheese recipe makes approximately 1 C. dip. What to do with any leftover dip? Just add a little water to thin it out and use as a dressing for salads! Just measure 2 T. of dip and then thin for nutritional info accuracy, per serving.

NET CARBS 1g - per serving (wings)				
calories	fat	protein	carbs	fiber
387	30g	27g	1g	0g

NET CARBS 1g - per serving (2 T. blue cheese dip)				
calories	fat	protein	carbs	fiber
149	15g	2g	1g	0g

Everything Crackers

It's pretty exciting to find a cracker that is low carb without tasting dry and bland. These crackers will rock your low-carb cracker world — and they're so much better than low carb store-bought crackers. My favorite way to eat these is spread with Lynda's Egg Salad, pg. 94, or served with sharp cheddar cheese slices. To make them even more flavorful, I add an 'Everything Seasoning' to the cracker batter that typically has sesame seeds, poppy seeds, garlic, dried onion, salt, etc. There are many brands on the market which are very easy to find online. Once you find your favorite brand, you will want to use it for 'everything' — including these crackers. If you don't have the seasoning and you want to make them right away, a little bit of garlic powder, dried rosemary, Italian seasoning, onion powder, or any other combination of flavors you enjoy will work just fine.

SERVINGS: 6

INGREDIENTS

1 ¾ C. blanched almond flour

¼ C. flaxseed meal

1 T. Everything seasoning

¼ tsp. xanthan gum

1 large egg, lightly beaten

DIRECTIONS

1. Preheat oven to 350 degrees.

2. Add dry ingredients to a medium bowl; stir to mix.

3. Add egg and stir with a fork until completely combined. Batter will be stiff.

4. Line a work surface with parchment paper, and place batter in center. Lay another piece of parchment paper over the top and roll to a rectangle 1/16" thick and approximately 12" x 14" inches overall – just do the best you can here; it doesn't have to be perfectly rectangular.

5. Remove top parchment paper and cut crackers into 1 ½" inch squares with a pizza cutter. Transfer bottom parchment paper with crackers on it to a baking sheet.

6. Bake 10 minutes. Remove from oven, separate crackers, and flip to other side. Bake an additional 8-10 minutes or just until crackers are starting to turn a light golden brown. (During baking, remove any crackers to the cooling rack that look to be done early; they will not all bake evenly.)

7. Transfer crackers to a cooling rack; cool completely. Crackers will become crisper as they cool. Store in an airtight container.

NET CARBS 2g - per serving (approximately 8 crackers)				
calories	fat	protein	carbs	fiber
242	20g	9g	7g	5g

Fiesta
Beef Nachos

SERVINGS: 4

This low carb version of nachos is full of flavor and fun to eat. I often make them for football game days, but they are great to make any day – I serve them as a snack or main meal. For larger crowds, the recipe may easily be doubled or tripled. Add toppings of choice to make the nachos to your liking.

INGREDIENTS

nachos

1 lb. tri-color mini sweet peppers

1 tsp. olive or avocado oil

½ lb. lean ground beef

1 chopped green onion

2 tsp. Taco Seasoning, pg. 128

1 C. shredded sharp cheddar cheese

1 fresh jalapeno, thinly sliced

toppings
(optional and to taste)

Mexican crema or sour cream

Chopped fresh cilantro

Easy Homestyle Salsa, pg. 121

Avocado Lime Crema, pg. 118

Sliced black olives

Chopped Roma tomatoes

Cubed avocado

DIRECTIONS

1. Preheat oven to 425 degrees.

2. Cut root ends off mini sweet peppers and discard. Slice peppers in half from tip-to-end; remove membrane and seeds. Discard.

3. Toss peppers in oil and place on a baking sheet, cut side up. Roast 5 minutes and remove from oven; set aside.

4. In a large skillet over medium/medium high heat, brown ground beef, onion and taco seasoning; drain.

5. Gather peppers close together on baking sheet, and sprinkle ground beef mixture evenly over peppers. Layer on cheese and sliced jalapeno.

6. Turn oven to broil, and place nachos 2–3" from heat. Broil 1–2 minutes or until cheese is melted.

7. Top with optional toppings, if desired. Eat with a fork or your fingers!

janeva's tips

Ground turkey or chicken may be subbed for the ground beef; adjust nutrition info as necessary.

NET CARBS 7g - per serving (no toppings)				
calories	fat	protein	carbs	fiber
186	11g	11g	9g	2g

Granola Bars
grain free

SERVINGS: 12

One cannot go wrong with a bar loaded with toasted coconut, a variety of nuts and some chocolate bits. I find that these cure the craving for a candy bar. Almond Joy® is my favorite candy, and these granola bars have a similar taste – best part is that it takes longer to chew them with all that nutty texture. One of my favorite snack treats!

INGREDIENTS

1 C. raw almonds, chopped

½ C. slivered almonds

½ C. chopped pecans

1 C. unsweetened coconut flakes, tightly packed

1 large egg

¼ C. allulose granular sugar substitute

2 T. natural almond butter, no added sugar

1 T. liquid coconut oil

¼ tsp. sea salt

¼ C. stevia chocolate chips (I use Lily's)

DIRECTIONS

1. Preheat oven to 375 degrees.

2. Line an 8" x 8" inch square baking pan with parchment paper leaving enough hanging over sides to easily lift bars out after baking.

3. Toast the nuts and coconut by spreading out on separate baking sheets. Bake according to bake time listed below. Bake just until lightly toasted – watch closely as they can burn quickly:

   Chopped almonds: bake 5-7 minutes

   Slivered almonds and chopped pecans: bake 3-5 minutes

   Coconut flakes: bake 2-4 minutes

4. Let nuts and coconut cool; reduce oven temp to 350 degrees.

5. Whisk egg and allulose in a large mixing bowl. In a separate bowl, whisk together the almond butter and coconut oil; add to egg mixture and whisk to blend.

6. Add nuts, coconut, salt and chocolate chips to egg mixture; mix until combined.

7. Add nut mixture to pan. Using a crumpled ball of parchment paper, (to prevent sticking to hands) press mixture into pan as firmly as possible. Failure to do so will result in crumbly bars!

8. Bake 15 minutes or until set. Cool completely and cut into 12 bars.

9. Store bars in an airtight container on counter for a few days; for a longer shelf life, store in refrigerator.

NET CARBS 1g - per serving				
calories	fat	protein	carbs	fiber
157	14g	4g	3g	2g

Guacamole Deviled Eggs

SERVINGS: 6
(2 egg halves serving size)

Creamy guacamole pairs well with eggs, and the avocado replaces the standard mayo found in the classic deviled eggs recipes. I like to purchase the eggs hard-boiled from the local grocer to make this snack a cinch to prepare. If you're up for making the hard-boiled eggs at home, see TIP.

INGREDIENTS

6 large hard-boiled eggs

2 ripe avocados, peeled and pitted

1 T. lime juice

1 T. sour cream

1 T. minced jalapeno (seeded and membrane removed)

1 T. chopped green onion

1 T. chopped fresh cilantro

¼ tsp. sea salt

DIRECTIONS

1. Slice hard-boiled eggs in half, lengthwise. Remove yolks; roughly chop 2 halves. Set chopped yolks and egg white halves aside. (Store remaining yolks in fridge for a later snack – they will not be needed for this recipe.)

2. Using a fork, mash avocados in a medium bowl. Add lime juice and mash to coat avocados (this will not only add flavor but help to prevent browning.) Add remaining ingredients (including chopped egg yolks), and mash to blend.

3. Generously fill egg white halves with avocado mixture using a heaping tablespoon.

4. Garnish filled eggs with additional cilantro leaves and minced or sliced jalapeno, if desired. Serve immediately.

janeva's tips

To hard boil eggs, add eggs to a medium saucepan. Fill with water covering eggs by 1" inch. Bring to a boil and continue to simmer 7- 8 minutes. Using a slotted spoon, transfer eggs to a bowl of ice-cold water. Cool a few minutes, and peel immediately; store covered in fridge until ready to use. Eggs may be prepared a few days in advance for this recipe. Guacamole should be made right before serving the deviled eggs as it will start to brown when exposed to air.

NET CARBS 2g - per serving				
calories	fat	protein	carbs	fiber
156	12g	7g	5g	3g

snacks & miscellaneous

Gummy
Fruit Chews

SERVINGS: 1

Bring back the kid in you by making this old-school treat. They're sweet and sour and perfect for a low carb and low-calorie snack.

INGREDIENTS

1 pkg. (.30 oz.) sugar free gelatin, any flavor (I use Jell-O®)

1 pkg. (.25 oz.) unflavored gelatin (I use Knox®)

¼ C. water

DIRECTIONS

1. Place a silicone gummy candy mold on a baking sheet. (Makes it easier to carry to refrigerator when filled.)

2. Add all ingredients to a small saucepan; stir. Heat over medium heat until gelatin is dissolved, stirring constantly.

3. Pour mixture into a vessel with a spout; I use a glass measuring cup.

4. Carefully pour mixture into silicone gummy candy mold. Refrigerate 40 minutes. Pop gummies out of mold; store in fridge until ready to eat.

janeva's tips

Total amount of gummies will vary depending on shape and mold used for making the chews. Amazon.com carries a wide variety of molds at a reasonable price.

NET CARBS 0g - per serving				
calories	fat	protein	carbs	fiber
15	0g	4g	0g	0g

Italian Sausage Stuffed Mushrooms

SERVINGS: 8

These filling appetizers are quick and easy – and just perfect for a gathering. I like to make them ahead, bake and freeze for times when a snack craving strikes, reheating just a few at a time instead of the entire batch. When ready to reheat them, thaw frozen mushrooms and reheat for 8-10 minutes at 350 degrees.

INGREDIENTS

16 oz. Italian bulk pork or turkey sausage

8 oz. cream cheese, softened

2 C. finely shredded cheddar cheese

½ tsp. red pepper flakes

1 lb. whole baby bella mushrooms, cleaned and stems removed

DIRECTIONS

1. Preheat oven to 425 degrees. Line a baking sheet with parchment paper; set aside.

2. Brown sausage in a skillet over medium/medium high heat. Drain and set aside.

3. In a bowl, mix together the cream cheese and cheddar cheese. Add red pepper flakes and sausage; mix.

4. Using a tablespoon or small cookie scoop, generously fill mushrooms.

5. Place stuffed mushrooms on baking sheet about 1" inch apart, (you may have to bake in batches) and bake 10-12 minutes or until lightly browned and mushrooms are cooked through.

janeva's tips

Servings may vary based on size of mushrooms; serving size and nutrition info is an estimate.

NET CARBS 2g - per serving (using turkey sausage)				
calories	fat	protein	carbs	fiber
269	20g	19g	3g	1g

snacks & miscellaneous

Nuts & Bolts
Celery

SERVINGS: 24
(½ stalk stuffed celery)

Move over potato chips! If you're looking for a savory snack, try this creamy, crunchy snack instead. I like to keep these filled celery sticks on hand in the fridge to control hunger pangs — they also make a great appetizer for a party or family gathering.

INGREDIENTS

12 celery stalks

8 oz. cream cheese, softened

2 T. heavy cream

1 C. sliced green olives with pimentos

1 T. chopped green onion

½ C. chopped pecans

½ C. chopped walnuts

DIRECTIONS

1. Wash and dry celery stalks; set aside.

2. Place cream cheese and heavy cream in a medium bowl; mix with an electric hand mixer on slow until creamy. Fold in olives, green onions and nuts.

3. Using a fork or table knife, fill celery stalks with cream cheese mixture; cut stalks in half and store covered in fridge.

NET CARBS 1g - per serving				
calories	fat	protein	carbs	fiber
80	8g	1g	1g	0g

snacks & miscellaneous

Spinach Artichoke Dip

SERVINGS: 10

This dip is a crowd favorite and equally delicious served hot or cold. Try it with pork rinds, fresh veggies, or low carb chips and crackers for dipping. If you're looking for a quick and easy chicken dish, just top some cooked chicken breasts with the dip and place under the broiler to melt.

INGREDIENTS

14 oz. can artichokes, drained and chopped

9 oz. pkg. frozen chopped spinach, thawed and squeezed to reduce liquid

8 oz. cream cheese, room temp

½ C. mayonnaise

½ C. sour cream

¼ tsp. salt

1/8 tsp. garlic powder

1/8 tsp. onion powder

1 ½ C. shredded parmesan cheese, divided

Cooking spray

DIRECTIONS

1. Preheat oven to 350 degrees.

2. Place all ingredients (except ½ C. of the parmesan cheese) in a large mixing bowl. Using a stand mixer or electric hand mixer, blend until mixed.

3. Spread mixture evenly in a sprayed 7" x 10" inch rectangular baking dish (you may also use a 9" inch glass pie plate or 8" x 8" inch square baking dish). Sprinkle with remaining ½ C. parmesan.

4. Bake 25-30 minutes or until cheese is lightly browned. Serve hot or cold.

NET CARBS 5g - per serving				
calories	fat	protein	carbs	fiber
229	20g	5g	7g	2g

snacks & miscellaneous

index

LISTED ALPHABETICALLY BY SECTION

acknowledgments

This cookbook is dedicated in memory of my son, Samuel Martin Eickhoff-Mazariego. You've taught me that the only way to fill an empty heart is to give and not to receive.

To my parents, I could fill every page of this book with gratitude for your encouragement, wisdom, support, and unconditional love every day of my life. To my mother, my mentor, and my favorite person on earth – thank you for the endless conversations both by phone and in person, pouring over the editing of this cookbook, listening to your soothing words of advice, and laughing so hard together we can't get a word out edgewise. Those memories will never fade. Your love of cooking and baking was truly passed down to me. I thank you for that gift of passion for the same, being able to do what I love to do. To my father, there are no words to express how much I miss you, yet I feel your presence with me and can 'hear' your words of wisdom and strength no matter.

To my siblings, you are an extension of our parents. Always offering an ear, a shoulder to lean on, and a reminder of the blessings we have been given. Thank you for your undying support.

To my friends, I'm blessed I'm unable to name all of you! For those who know about my endeavor, you've been a part of my journey and a tremendous support. Thank you for understanding those failed commitments or time together in this season of my life. I know by the time you read this, we will have toasted a time or two.

To my social media followers, it is truly you who drive me to create recipes to provide a fun, interesting and tasty low carb lifestyle. Many of you feel like family even though we've never met. Thank you for your continued support and positive feedback – it lights my passion to help where I can, so we all succeed at this lifestyle.

To my professional connections including 26 Projects and Friesen's Corporation – you're all just awesome people to work with and have played a key part in helping to master my vision of this enormous and enjoyable project.

— janeva